Django 1.0 Template Development

A practical guide to Django template development
with custom tags, filters, multiple templates, caching,
and more

Scott Newman

BIRMINGHAM - MUMBAI

Django 1.0 Template Development

First published: December 2008

Production Reference: 1051208

Published by Packt Publishing Ltd.
32 Lincoln Road
Olton
Birmingham, B27 6PA, UK.

ISBN 978-1-847195-70-8

www.packtpub.com

Cover Image by Vinayak Chittar (vinayak.chittar@gmail.com)

Credits

Author

Scott Newman

Reviewers

Jan V Smith

Dave Fregon

Patrick Chan

Senior Acquisition Editor

Douglas Paterson

Development Editor

Ved Prakash Jha

Technical Editors

Abhinav Prasoon

John Antony

Copy Editor

Sneha Kulkarni

Editorial Team Leader

Mithil Kulkarni

Project Manager

Abhijeet Deobhakta

Project Coordinator

Leena Purkait

Indexer

Rekha Nair

Proofreader

Chris Smith

Production Coordinator

Aparna Bhagat

Cover Work

Aparna Bhagat

About the Author

Scott Newman has been developing commercial web sites since 1997. Since then, he has professionally developed web applications in C, PERL, ColdFusion, ASP, PHP, and Python. He has also been a Windows network administrator and desktop application developer, but always gravitates back to web development. Scott holds a Network+ certification and is a dotMobi Certified Mobile Web Developer.

In recent years, Scott worked as the system development manager for a major media company developing CMS and mobile applications in Django. He currently is the consulting director for the Big Nerd Ranch in Atlanta, GA.

I would like to thank my wife, Jennifer, for her patience, support, and encouragement during the months it took to write this book — I could not have done it without her. I would also like to thank Jon-Paul Roden and Patrick Ward for helping me become the programmer I am today. A big thanks to Jim Riley and Rusty Coats for getting me involved in Django, believing in my crazy idea to write a CMS from scratch, and supporting my team along the way. Finally, I would like to thank my mom and dad for always being there for me.

About the Reviewers

Jan V Smith has been working on open source software since 2001. She is based in Melbourne, Australia. Jan is Vice President of Computerbank Victoria. Computerbank takes donated computers and refurbishes them with Ubuntu and open source software and then distributes them to people on low incomes. She has reviewed several open source Python-based text books.

> Thanks to my son Michael Cassidy for wanting to learn HTML in 1999. We studied HTML together, later I discovered the vast possibilities of the open source software movement. A movement where intelligence and kindness coexist to help overcome short sighted, greedy vendor lock-in.

Dave Fregon has been working with Zope since 1999, and open source concepts since 1996, and 'most all of his general work is in this area, recently adding Django to his growing repertoir. Dave has contributed to projects such as the engagemedia. org and axxs.org community hosting services, among many other web-enabling community efforts outside of his commercial work. It keeps him busy when he is not out exploring the bush and rivers of Australia with his dog, Shade.

An active member of the Australian Zope community OzZope, Dave co-wrote a chapter on Zope security with another member Jan Smith, for the book "Zope—Content Management Systems and Beyond" edited by Stephan Richter, released in German.

After working many years as contractor, he joined with others in regional Australia to form a workers collective, NetAxxs.com.au, which provides Python-friendly web hosting and development in Open Source technologies, as well as free servers for community and activist-based hosting.

I'd like to thank all the contributors to open source projects, that have given me inspiration in life and push me to contributing more to the commons, the author amongst them. For my brother Peter who inspired me with geekdom, to Karen for dealing with me in the office, Shade for dealing with me all the time, and Leena Purkait from Packt Publishing for her patience during a time of illness for me whilst contributing to this books release.

Patrick Chan has recently survived a bachelor of computer engineering with honors.

He is now an analyst programmer with Australia Post and also volunteers at Computer Bank. Along with Jan Smith, he is working on ComputerbankDB, a Django project that would replace the current inventory system for Computer Bank.

Patrick finds that unlike many other languages (names withheld to protect the guilty), you don't tend to have to pull your hair out if you are programming in Python. In fact, you have to be careful because you might actually find it fun and enjoyable.

Table of Contents

Preface

Django is a high-level Python web application framework designed to support the rapid development of dynamic web sites, web applications, and web services. It includes a template system that allows programmers and designers to easily and efficiently output their content in a flexible, extendable, and maintainable manner.

This book is a comprehensive, practical exploration of Django's template system. Developers and template authors will appreciate the introduction to Django templates, including an examination of views, generic views, and URL configurations to illustrate how incoming requests are handled and ultimately mapped to templates. Template inheritance and outputting different templates based on user agents are also covered.

The chapters on pagination, internationalization, caching, and customizing the admin application are example-driven so you can learn the concepts and later apply them as "recipes" in your own projects. For most examples, we will be working with an ongoing example project to show the power of combining your new skills together.

Whether large or small, complex or simple, I hope the techniques presented in this book serve you well in your Django projects.

What this book covers

Here is a brief summary of each chapter:

Chapter 1 gives you an introduction to the Django template system and provides an overview of how it works.

Chapter 2 explores how URL configuration routes your requests to views and generic views. You will understand how to use generic views to streamline your project's development.

Chapter 3 explains how data from your views is exposed to the template system via the template context.

Chapter 4 reviews all of Django's built-in tags and filters, each with examples and usage notes.

Chapter 5 uses extension and inheritance to create a modular skeleton for your project's templates.

Chapter 6 teaches you how to serve multiple versions of your templates in a single Django project. You will create mobile and traditional templates and learn how to serve them from the same views.

Chapter 7 explains how to extend the template system by writing your own template tags and filters.

Chapter 8 teaches you how to use Django's pagination libraries to split the output of your applications into pages and provide navigation between them.

Chapter 9 shows you how to customize the look and feel of the automatic admin application by editing some templates and creating custom CSS rules.

Chapter 10 teaches you to use the cache framework to optimize the speed and performance of your project.

Chapter 11 uses internationalization to automatically serve your site templates in multiple languages based on the user's preferences.

What you need for this book

- A working installation of Python 2.3 or greater (2.4 or greater is recommended)

- The ability to run a Django-supported database (examples in the book use SQLite)

- An installed and working Django installation (see `www.DjangoProject.com` for installation details)

- Some experience with Django, at least having gone through the tutorials at `www.DjangoProject.com`

Who this book is for

This book is for web developers and template authors who want to fully understand and utilize the Django template system. The reader should have completed the introductory tutorials on the Django project's web site and some experience with the framework will be very helpful. Basic knowledge of Python and HTML is assumed.

Conventions

In this book, you will find a number of styles of text that distinguish between different kinds of information. Here are some examples of these styles, and an explanation of their meaning.

Code words in text are shown as follows: "We can include other contexts through the use of the `include` directive."

A block of code will be set as follows:

```
{% ifequal color 'blue' %}
  Wow, you like blue!
{% else %}
  Why don't you like blue?
{% endifequal %}
```

When we wish to draw your attention to a particular part of a code block, the relevant lines or items will be made bold:

```
from django.http import HttpResponse
from django.template import Context, Template, loader
def detail(request):
    dict_values = {'fav_color': 'blue'}
    template_string = "My favorite color is {{ fav_color }}."
    c = Context(dict_values)
    t = Template(template_string)
    rendered_template = t.render(c)
    return HttpResponse(rendered_template)
```

Any command-line input and output is written as follows:

```
$ python manage.py runserver
```

New terms and **important words** are introduced in a bold-type font. Words that you see on the screen, in menus or dialog boxes for example, appear in our text like this: "clicking the **Next** button moves you to the next screen".

Warnings or important notes appear in a box like this.

 Tips and tricks appear like this.

Reader feedback

Feedback from our readers is always welcome. Let us know what you think about this book, what you liked or may have disliked. Reader feedback is important for us to develop titles that you really get the most out of.

To send us general feedback, simply drop an email to feedback@packtpub.com, making sure to mention the book title in the subject of your message.

If there is a book that you need and would like to see us publish, please send us a note in the **SUGGEST A TITLE** form on www.packtpub.com or email suggest@packtpub.com.

If there is a topic that you have expertise in and you are interested in either writing or contributing to a book, see our author guide on www.packtpub.com/authors.

Customer support

Now that you are the proud owner of a Packt book, we have a number of things to help you to get the most from your purchase.

Downloading the example code for the book

Visit http://www.packtpub.com/files/code/5708_Code.zip to directly download the example code.

 The downloadable files contain instructions on how to use them.

Errata

Although we have taken every care to ensure the accuracy of our contents, mistakes do happen. If you find a mistake in one of our books—maybe a mistake in text or code—we would be grateful if you would report this to us. By doing this you can save other readers from frustration, and help to improve subsequent versions of this book. If you find any errata, report them by visiting `http://www.packtpub.com/support`, selecting your book, clicking on the **let us know** link, and entering the details of your errata. Once your errata are verified, your submission will be accepted and the errata added to the list of existing errata. The existing errata can be viewed by selecting your title from `http://www.packtpub.com/support`.

Piracy

Piracy of copyright material on the Internet is an ongoing problem across all media. At Packt, we take the protection of our copyright and licenses very seriously. If you come across any illegal copies of our works in any form on the Internet, please provide the location address or web site name immediately so we can pursue a remedy.

Please contact us at `copyright@packtpub.com` with a link to the suspected pirated material.

We appreciate your help in protecting our authors, and our ability to bring you valuable content.

Questions

You can contact us at `questions@packtpub.com` if you are having a problem with some aspect of the book, and we will do our best to address it.

1

An Introduction to the Django Template System

Django simplifies the process of creating data-driven applications and provides a flexible, modular approach to web development. In contrast to many other web application frameworks, Django is full stack, which means it contains all the libraries and packages necessary to create applications. Because the pieces were designed as a whole, you can develop using them with the confidence that they will all work well together. One of these pieces is the Django template system that allows output to be formatted in a flexible, consistent, and maintainable fashion.

In this chapter we will:

- Learn what templates are and why you should use them
- Review how Django handles requests
- Learn the syntax used in the templating system
- Set up a demo application that we will use throughout this book

What are templates?

The term *template* can have different meanings depending on what programming environment, language, or framework you are working in, so let's clarify what it represents to Django developers. In Django, a template is a string that can be combined with data to produce output. Typically, templates are stored as files on the file system, and contain placeholders that are replaced with information from the database and the results returned as HTML documents.

Understanding the need for templates

In some development platforms, such as PHP and ASP, the programming code and the HTML markup is all contained in a single file that gets processed and returned by the web server. In complex pages, this approach can become difficult to develop and maintain because there isn't a separation between the presentation and the programming logic used to render it.

Having programming logic mixed in with your markup code also limits the ability for designers to work in the files, unless they also understand the bits of programming logic sprinkled within. This makes changing the markup both tedious and time-consuming because the developer usually has to do the updates.

This clearly isn't a productive way to develop applications. We end up with a number of requirements that need to be addressed:

- We need to separate the output markup from the Python code
- The system should encourage reusability and maintainability of output files
- Common page elements should be contained in their own files and easily included into the overall structure of the site
- Designers and developers need to be able to work without getting in each other's way
- The system should have a shallow learning curve and only require a basic understanding of programming concepts
- The system needs to be extensible and flexible enough to fit the specific needs of our projects

Overview of the Django template system

The Django template system fits all of these criteria nicely. By separating code and content, allowing only basic programming constructs, and making it possible to write your own extensions to the system, the Django authors have created a solution that works well for both designers and developers.

Separating code from presentation

Instead of mixing programming code and presentation markup (such as HTML) in the same files, we create templates that have placeholders where the data will go. When the template engine renders the templates, these placeholders are replaced with their appropriate values. By the time the output is returned to the web browser, all traces of the template have been removed, leaving only the resulting output.

As we have seen, Django templates, typically, are files loaded by the template engine and rendered into output that will be sent back to the browser. This loading and rendering takes place in the **view**, the function that Django calls to fulfill requests.

 In some web development frameworks, the terms **view** and **template** are used differently. In Django, the view is a Python function that is called by the framework to return an HTTP response. The template is a file or string that encapsulates the presentation markup that is used to generate the response.

In order to accomplish basic output logic, such as looping through records and creating table rows, some programming code needs to exist in the template files. The amount of programming you can do in your template depends on your programming language or framework; Django allows basic looping and conditional logic. The process of rendering executes this template logic and replaces placeholders with data.

Helping designers and developers collaborate

By separating templates out of framework code into their own files, developers and designers can work simultaneously on the same project without stepping on each other's work. This approach has the added benefit that there is a clear differentiation between design and development; coders stay out of the design arena and designers stay out of the programming arena—we can live in harmony! (Well, maybe...)

Keeping the template clear of code also makes it easier to work in WYSIWYG (What You See Is What You Get) editors such as Dreamweaver and Homesite. We're not going to cover that in the book, but it's worth mentioning.

Increasing maintainability

The template files are usually located in their own folders nested somewhere in the Django project. The templates can include other templates in them, and so common page elements such as menus, headers, and footers can be kept in their own files. Including common elements from single files increases the maintainability of our application by reducing the amount of common output markup that is duplicated in different files. Instead of hunting around for all the occurrences of some HTML to replace, we can make the change in one place and all templates that include the content will be updated automatically.

Templates can also have parent templates that simplify the development of sections of a site. For example, if we have a calendar listing in the events section of a website, we might use three templates:

- A child template that handles the listing of calendar items
- A parent template that handles the formatting of the events section of the site
- A grandparent template that handles the formatting of the overall site

This prevents the duplication of site- and section-wide HTML by keeping them in single files. We'll explore the parent-child relationship and inheritance of templates in great detail in a later chapter.

Template syntax

The syntax of the template system is intentionally clean, simple, and elegant. With a minimal understanding of programming concepts, you can make powerful and flexible templates to output your data.

We'll cover these concepts and the syntax of the template language later in this chapter.

Modularity and reusability

Django ships with many built-in template elements that we can use to control and format the output of our templates. You can also write your own template elements, if you have a need that isn't met by the default libraries, or use ones that other developers have written. Sites such as `DjangoSnippets.org` contain many template libraries that developers have shared and can be easily incorporated into your own site.

In a later chapter, we'll cover writing your own template element libraries and how to install and use libraries that others have written.

Flexibility

The template system is flexible enough so that we can output any kind of data that we want. It doesn't assume (or require) that you are going to produce HTML. We can dynamically generate PDF documents, CSV files, HTML files, microformats, and text documents. It also doesn't require you to write your templates in any specific format (such as XML) the way some other Python templating languages do.

Even though you can extend the template system with custom elements to fit your needs, the Django creators gave us the ultimate back door—You don't have to use their template system! You are free to implement any Python template system and libraries of your choice, and you can do it on an as-needed basis in only the places you desire. For example, if you want to use the Django template system for half of your views and the open-source Genshi templating system for the other half, there's no penalty.

Limitations

The elegance and simplicity of the Django template system comes at a price; there are a few limitations to be aware of. In a nutshell, only the processing of simple presentation logic is supported in templates. You can loop over sets of data and check the value of objects and variables to perform conditional logic, but you cannot perform complex logic and execute raw Python code.

Here are a few things you cannot do using the Django template system syntax:

- You cannot execute arbitrary Python code inside a template.
- You cannot set or modify the value of variables inside a template.
- You cannot pass arguments to the methods of objects inside a template.

If you need to perform these kinds of actions, you can often write your own extensions to the template system. We will fully cover these limitations and their implications later in the book.

Critics of the system

Some critics argue that the Django template system is too simple and isn't robust enough to perform complex formatting or outputting. This may be true, but remember that these limitations are intentional to achieve the design goals we discussed earlier. You're also free not to use Django's template system and use a more liberal template library if you choose.

Personally, after using Django's template system on a team of designers and developers for almost two years, I find that the simplicity and elegance of the system results in disciplined application design. This simplicity enforces consistency in the templates, and makes developers consider the output and prepare their data properly before sending it off to the templates to be rendered. This prevents logic from creeping into the templates as deadlines start to loom and developers cut corners to meet them! (Not that any of us would do that, of course!)

Exploring how Django handles requests

In order to understand how the template system works in conjunction with the rest of the Django framework, we should briefly explore how a request is handled. Understanding this process isn't critical to working with templates, but it will help you make sense of what is happening. This isn't an exhaustive explanation, but it should get us through a basic understanding of what is happening beneath the covers.

Here's how a typical request is handled:

1. A URL is requested.
2. The middleware is called.
3. The URL is evaluated.
4. The middleware is called (again).
5. The view is called.
6. The template object and template file are loaded.
7. The template is rendered.
8. The middleware is called (yet again).
9. The output is sent to the browser.

```
┌─────────────────────────────────────────────────┐
│  ┌─────────────────────────────────────────────┐ │
│  │   The incoming HTTP request is received      │ │
│  └─────────────────────────────────────────────┘ │
│                       ⇩                           │
│  ┌─────────────────────────────────────────────┐ │
│  │  Middleware is called (Request preprocessor) │ │
│  └─────────────────────────────────────────────┘ │
│                       ⇩                           │
│  ┌─────────────────────────────────────────────┐ │
│  │    URL Matched against list of patterns      │ │
│  └─────────────────────────────────────────────┘ │
│                       ⇩                           │
│  ┌─────────────────────────────────────────────┐ │
│  │   Middleware is called (View preprocessor)   │ │
│  └─────────────────────────────────────────────┘ │
│                       ⇩                           │
│  ┌─────────────────────────────────────────────┐ │
│  │               View is called                │ │
│  └─────────────────────────────────────────────┘ │
│                       ⇩                           │
│  ┌─────────────────────────────────────────────┐ │
│  │       Template is loaded and rendered        │ │
│  └─────────────────────────────────────────────┘ │
│                       ⇩                           │
│  ┌─────────────────────────────────────────────┐ │
│  │ Middleware is called (Response preprocessor) │ │
│  └─────────────────────────────────────────────┘ │
│                       ⇩                           │
│  ┌─────────────────────────────────────────────┐ │
│  │        HTTP response is returned             │ │
│  └─────────────────────────────────────────────┘ │
└─────────────────────────────────────────────────┘
```

Step 1: A URL is requested

The user requests a web page via URL in his/her browser. The web server receives this request and passes it to Python and Django.

 Note: We are skipping over the gritty details of DNS, routing, web server interface to Python, and so on. Those are way out of the scope of the book, so just take for granted that Django has received the request properly.

Step 2: The middleware is called

Django has a special mechanism called the middleware that allows you to call functions at a number of places in this request-response cycle. You can invoke a middleware function in four places: before the URL resolution, before the view is called, after the view is called, and if the view raises an exception (if there's a problem).

 The middleware at this step is called the **Request Preprocessor**, but that's extra-credit information.

Step 3: The URL is evaluated

Django's URL dispatcher compares the requested URL with a list of patterns (regular expressions, to be exact). If a match is found, Django imports and calls the view that is associated with the pattern. This process is known as **URL resolution**.

The view is a Python function that handles the creation of the response. If additional pieces of data have been sent in the URL (such as product IDs, story names, and so on), they are passed as arguments to the function.

 Django also has a concept called **Generic Views** that can automatically load and render a template at this step without having to go any further. We'll look at generic views in a later chapter.

Step 4: The middleware is called (again)

If you have middleware functions to be run after URL resolution but before the view is executed, it will be called here.

 The middleware at this step is called the **View Preprocessor**.

Step 5: The view is called

The view is where the rubber meets the road, so to speak.

The majority of views will use the database API to perform some kind of **CRUD** (**create, retrieve, update**, and **delete**) operation, load a template, render the output, and send it back to the user.

The Python code in the view function is executed at this point. Usually this entails retrieving some kind of data, most often by using the Django database API to retrieve model objects.

Once the data is retrieved, it is passed to a special object called the Context. This is the object that holds the retrieved data and makes it available to the templates. For now, think of it as a dictionary of variable names and values that the template will get. If you are not familiar with Python dictionaries, see the code notes later in this chapter or look in the Python standard documentation.

Models are not required in views, nor is even having a database! Of course, that would be kind of silly, since we're trying to create a data-driven site. It should just be stated that you don't HAVE to have a model to have a valid view.

Step 6: The template object and template file are loaded

The template object is called and gets the appropriate template file from the file system at the location specified in the view. This relative path is combined with the templates directory specified in our project's `settings.py` file.

As we discussed earlier in the chapter, templates are not technically required to send back responses, but they make your life much easier. We'll see this in the upcoming examples in this chapter.

Step 7: The template is rendered

The text inside the template is rendered. The placeholders are replaced with their associated data and statements of template logic (such as looping) are performed. At this point, the rendered template is just a large Python string of characters.

Step 8: The middleware is called (again)

If you have middleware functions to be run after the response is generated but before it's sent back to the user, they are called at this step.

The middleware at this step is called the **Response Postprocessor**.

Step 9: The output is sent to the browser

The rendered template is packaged up with formatting that is needed by the browser to understand how to accept and display the page. By adding this formatting, the string has been turned into an HTTP response that is sent back to the browser.

In this example, the response is HTML, but it doesn't have to be. It could also be plain text, XML, JavaScript, CSV, PDF, and so on. Part of the formatting of the HTTP response tells the browser what the MIME type of the response is, and it tells the browser what kind of data to expect.

Understanding the template system syntax

Now that we have a basic understanding of how the template system fits into the big picture, we can finally explore some basics of how it works.

As we discussed earlier, Django templates are basically just text files that have placeholders and simple logic in them. These placeholders are evaluated when the template is rendered, and Django replaces them with the values that go in their place.

Let's illustrate with a quick example of a template file:

```
<html>
<head>
<title>{{ page_title }}</title>
</head>
<body>
<h1>{{ header }}</h1>
{% for name in names_list %}
{{ name.last|upper }}, {{ name.first|upper }}<br/>
{% endfor %}
</body>
</html>
```

Don't worry if you don't immediately grasp these concepts. We'll be running through a practical example of the syntax at the end of the chapter.

Context variable

If you recall the request-handling overview, we said the context was a special object that contained the values available to the template when it is rendered. We'll work through a practical example later in the chapter. For now, just think of it as a dictionary of variables that the template will be able to see (see the upcoming code note if you don't know what a Python dictionary is).

Variables

Variables are the basic placeholders in a Django template. They are identified by two curly brackets on each side:

```
My favorite color is {{ color }}.
```

When the Django template engine renders this page, it will see {{ color }} as a placeholder for the real value it is supposed to put in its place. It looks in the context for a key named `color` and finds the value associated. If our context has a key named `color` and an associated value of `blue`, the output would look like this:

My favorite color is blue.

Filters

Filters can format the output of variables in Django templates. They are identified by the use of a pipe symbol immediately following a template variable:

```
My favorite color is {{ color|upper }}.
```

In this example, `upper` is the filter we are using to modify the variable `color`. (Notice there is no space between the variable, the pipe, and the filter.) The `upper` filter will take the value of the variable and convert all the letters to upper case. (Specifically, it applies the Python string function `upper()` to the value.) Here is the resulting output:

```
My favorite color is BLUE.
```

 The filters don't change the value of the variables they modify, but just modify the way they are outputted. In our example, if you use {{ color }} somewhere else in your template without the template filter, it won't appear in upper case.

Django ships with a number of default filters that cover many common presentation-formatting needs. You can find them listed in the Django documentation at `DjangoProject.com`.

Tags

Template tags instruct the template rendering engine to perform some kind of action. They are identified by a curly bracket and percentage symbol, and often have an accompanying closing tag:

```
{% ifequal color 'blue' %}
   Wow, you like blue!
```

```
{% else %}
  Why don't you like blue?
{% endifequal %}
```

In this example, we are using the template tag `ifequal`. It takes two arguments, which means the values to be compared. Unlike Python code, we don't use parentheses or commas around the arguments. We just use a space between the template tag and each of the arguments. The tag also has a corresponding closing tag `endifequal` that tells the template engine we are done.

In this example, since the value of the variable is `blue`, we get this output:

Wow, you like blue!

Like filters, Django ships with a number of default tags that perform common logic in templates such as looping through sets of data. We'll be covering tags and filters in more depth in later chapters as well as writing our own custom tags.

When the templates are rendered, the tags are removed by the template engine. If you view the source of your output, you will not see your tags, though you will probably see a blank space where the tag was.

Comments

There are two kinds of comments we can use in Django templates: single-line and multi-line. Like comments in Python, you can leave yourself notes in a template or use comments to prevent a chunk of template code from being rendered by the template engine. Single-line comments are identified by a curly bracket and a hash mark (also known as the number sign or pound symbol):

```
{# Remember to move this down the page later #}
My favorite color is {{ color }}.
```

Multi-line comments are implemented as tags, and they have a corresponding `endcomment` tag:

```
{% comment %}
{% ifequal color 'blue' %}
  Wow, you like blue!
{% else %}
  Why don't you like blue?
{% endifequal %}
{% endcomment %}
```

In this example, the template engine ignores everything between the `comment` and `endcomment` tags. This is often used to troubleshoot and debug a section of template that isn't behaving properly.

Like template tags, single- and multi-line comments are removed from the resulting output by the template engine. They are not the same as HTML comments; you won't see them if you view the source of your output.

Code note: Python dictionaries

In case you are not familiar with Python dictionaries, here is a basic explanation.

A dictionary is one of Python's built-in data types, similar to hashes in other programming languages. It consists of keys and values. The key is the label used to identify the item, and the value is what it is equal to.

Here's an example:

```
>> mydictionary = {}
>> mydictionary['mykey'] = 'myvalue'
>> mydictionary['myotherkey'] = 10
>> print mydictionary
{'mykey': 'myvalue', 'myotherkey': 10}
```

The first line tells Python that we are creating a new dictionary called `mydictionary`. The empty curly brackets tell Python that we are creating a variable that is of type dictionary and not a string or integer. The next two lines add keys and values to the dictionary. The first adds a new key called `mykey` that has a value of `myvalue`. The second has a key of `myotherkey` and has a value of `10`.

 We can mix numbers and strings as values of the keys. They don't all have to be the same type.

You can also create a dictionary in one step:

```
>> mydictionary = {'mykey': 'myvalue', 'myotherkey': 10}
```

This may look a little more complex, but it does the same thing the first three lines of our example above did.

Why is all of this important? It lets us keep all of our values grouped under a single variable. In the Django template language, the Context holds a dictionary of all the values we are going to make available to our template. When Django passes the dictionary to the template, the keys are what the placeholders are going to work with to be replaced with their values.

How invalid variables are handled

If you try to use a variable in your template that has not been made available to the context object, you will not get an error. The template system simply ignores it and keeps on going. This was a design decision by the Django developers to prevent a missing data item from "breaking" an application.

If you have an error with a template tag, however, you will get an error.

Creating our demo application

Throughout the book, we're going to work with the same example site so that we don't have to set up a new project for every chapter. This project will explore all the concepts throughout the book.

Rather than work with the clichéd example of a blog, we'll work with example applications that you'd find in a typical corporate website, such as news and press releases. If you've ever worked a corporate job, you've probably done something like this (and if you haven't, stick it on your resume when you're done!).

The specific configuration directives (project file system locations, database names/passwords, and so on) are given to maintain consistency throughout the book. Feel free to change them to suit your specific needs, but be sure your `settings.py` file matches your setup. If you decide to put the project in a different directory on the file system than what is used here, make sure to change your code appropriately when doing the examples in this book. (Hint: It's probably easier to follow along with these values if at all possible!)

Prerequisite #1: Install and test the Django framework

Installing the Django framework is thoroughly covered in the documentation on the `DjangoProject.com` site. If you have trouble, you can try posting a message to the **Django-Users | Google Group** (`http://groups-beta.google.com/group/ django-users`).

If you can start a Python shell and successfully run the command `import django`, you should be good to continue.

 At the time of this writing, the latest release of Django is 1.0, so that's what we will be using here.

Prerequisite #2: Create a new database

For purposes of this book, it doesn't matter what database engine you use as long as Django supports it (for example, MySQL, PostgreSQL, SQLite, and so on). If you don't have MySQL or PostgreSQL installed, SQLite is probably the easiest choice to work with as it requires zero administration to set up and use.

If you are using MySQL or PostgreSQL, following the instructions of your specific database engine, perform the following tasks. (If you are using SQLite, you don't have to do this.)

1. Create a database called mycompany.
2. Create a user called mycompany with a password of mycompany.

Step 1: Create the Project Directory

Create a file system location for our Django project files. This is one of the couple of places where your settings might vary depending on the operating system you are using:

For Unix/Mac: Create a /projects/ directory.

For Windows: Create a c:\projects\ directory.

Step 2: Start your project

From the projects directory, run this command:

```
$ django-admin.py startproject mycompany
```

This will create a mycompany directory under projects.

Note: Rather than writing out both Windows and Mac/Linux versions of the full filesystem path each time we refer to it, the directory will be referred to as mycompany/ instead of /projects/mycompany or c:\projects\mycompany. If you see mycompany/, you can safely assume that we are talking about those directories.

Step 3: Test your installation

In the mycompany directory, run this command:

```
$ python manage.py runserver
```

Browse to http://localhost:8000 and make sure you see the blue **It Worked!** screen.

During development and testing, you will have to keep starting and stopping the development web server. Anytime you need to browse a URL to test your application, you need to have the server running. Some people like to keep it running in a separate terminal window during development. Just be aware that the web server will restart each time you change a file. If you have a typo in your saved file, the web server may stop and display an error message and you'll need to manually stop and start the web server again when this happens.

Step 4: Configure the project's settings

For the upcoming chapters, we need to make sure Django is configured to use our database. In the mycompany/settings.py file, edit the database settings to match what you are using:

```
DATABASE_ENGINE = 'sqlite3'
DATABASE_NAME = '/projects/mycompany/mycompany.db'
DATABASE_USER = ''
DATABASE_PASSWORD = ''
DATABASE_HOST = ''
DATABASE_PORT = ''
```

The settings above are valid if you are using SQLite, which is preferable because it requires no configuration. If you are using a different database engine, such PostgreSQL or MySQL, make sure you configure the settings accordingly. Consult the online documentation if you are having trouble.

Starting our application

We now have an empty skeleton of a project upon which we can start building applications. The first application we are going to work with will just be a demonstration to get us warmed up.

Step 1: Create the demo project

In the mycompany directory, run this command:

```
$ python manage.py startapp demo
```

This will create a demo directory under the mycompany directory.

Step 2: Add a detail function to the demo view

In the file mycompany/demo/views.py, add these lines:

```
from django.http import HttpResponse

def detail(request):
    return HttpResponse('got here!')
```

Step 3: Add a URL pattern for our demo project

In the file mycompany/urls.py, edit the file to look like this:

```
from django.conf.urls.defaults import *

urlpatterns = patterns('',
    (r'^demo/$', 'mycompany.demo.views.detail'),
)
```

This tells the URL dispatcher that if it matches a URL of http://localhost:8000/demo/, call the detail function inside the file mycompany/demo/views.py.

 The URL dispatcher automatically strips the http://localhost:8000/ portion when matching, so we don't need to include it as part of our pattern.

Step 4: Make sure it worked

In the mycompany directory, run this command:

$ python manage.py runserver

This will start the Django development server. You should see something very similar to the following:

```
Validating models...
0 errors found
Django version 1.0-final-SVN-unknown, using settings 'mycompany.
settings'
Development server is running at http://127.0.0.1:8000/
Quit the server with CONTROL-C.
```

Browse to http://localhost:8000/demo/. You should see the **got here!** line we wrote in our view.

Congratulations! We've created our first Django view. We've built a solid base to start from and we're ready to start playing with views, contexts, and (of course!) templates.

Adding templates to our application

The app we built in the last section serves a page, but it's only a starting point for the application we are going to build. Let's use it to explore some concepts of how Django templates work.

Adding variables to the view

Before we start loading templates, we need to explore the Context and Template objects. As we discussed, the context makes variables and objects available to the templates during rendering. We pass it a dictionary of variables and objects and their associated values. When the template is rendered, the placeholders will be replaced with their corresponding values.

Edit your mycompany/demo/views.py file, adding the highlighted line and replacing your detail function with this one:

```
from django.http import HttpResponse
from django.template import Context, Template, loader

def detail(request):
    dict_values = {'fav_color': 'blue'}
    template_string = "My favorite color is {{ fav_color }}."
    c = Context(dict_values)
    t = Template(template_string)
    rendered_template = t.render(c)
    return HttpResponse(rendered_template)
```

Browse to http://localhost:8000/demo/ and you should see the simple one-liner response:

My favorite color is blue.

So what happened here? Let's break it down.

We created a simple dictionary called dict_values and populated a key called fav_color with a value of blue. If you're not familiar with Python dictionary syntax, check out the code note earlier in this chapter or the Python standard documentation under 'Data Structures'. You'll want to be familiar with this syntax; it's used quite a bit with Django.

We also created a string named template_string that contains our first taste of the Django template syntax. The double brackets in the string are simply the delimiter used to identify template variables. {{ fav_color }} tells the template rendering function that this is a placeholder for the value of the variable fav_color.

Next, we created a context object named c and passed it our dictionary. We also created a template object called t and passed it our template string.

 Templates don't have to be stored as files, they can also be strings. When you load a template, Django opens the file and extracts the text into a variable. We're keeping the example simple to start with here and just using a string to represent our template.

When we call the `render` method of the `Template` object, it parses the template string and replaces any template variables and logic with the appropriate values. In this case, `{{ fav_color }}` was replaced with the value `blue`. The rendered template is returned as a string to the `rendered_template` variable.

Finally, we send the value of the variable `rendered_template` to the browser as an HTTP response. Django nicely handles all the necessary steps of properly formatting the output for the browser to do its work and displaying the HTML.

Keep in mind that the verbosity of this example is intentional to keep the example clear. If you are familiar with Python, you'll know it could be written more concisely like this:

```
def detail(request):
    c = Context({'fav_color': 'blue'})
    t = Template("My favorite color is {{ fav_color }}.")
    return HttpResponse(t.render(c))
```

Moving the logic into a separate template file

Templates are usually longer than five words, so let's put the template string into a separate file.

We need to create a `templates` directory in our project. Technically, the templates could go anywhere on the file system, but it is common to put them under a `templates` directory at the root of your project. Create a directory called `templates` under the `mycompany` directory.

In your `mycompany/settings.py` file, find the `TEMPLATE_DIRS` variable (it's actually a Python tuple) and add a reference to our new `templates` directory:

```
TEMPLATE_DIRS = (
    '/projects/mycompany/templates/',
)
```

 In Windows, use the value `c:/projects/mycompany/templates/`. The slashes don't follow the normal Windows syntax, but it's what Django requires.

Even though we are only specifying a single directory of templates, make sure you have the trailing comma after the file path in `TEMPLATE_DIRS`. If you omit it, Python will treat your `TEMPLATE_DIRS` variable as a string, not a tuple, and you'll get an error when you try to run it.

Adding a trailing comma in a list or tuple is also good practice since Python allows trailing commas. If you always leave a comma after your last item, you won't forget to add it the next time you add another item to the end of the sequence.

While we are in the `settings.py` file, let's enable debugging for our project by setting the `DEBUG` and `TEMPLATE_DEBUG` variables at the top of the file to `True`:

```
DEBUG = True
TEMPLATE_DEBUG = True
```

This will ensure that Django shows us error pages with debugging information instead of a blank page.

Now that we've told Django where to find the templates, let's create a file called `example.html` in the `mycompany/templates` directory. In the file, add the line that was in our `detail` view:

```
My favorite color is {{ fav_color }}.
```

We need to change our view to load this new template file. Edit your `mycompany/demo/views.py` file and change the `detail` view to look like this:

```
def detail(request):
    c = Context({ 'fav_color': 'blue' })
    t = loader.get_template('example.html')
    rendered_template = t.render(c)
    return HttpResponse(rendered_template)
```

Browse to `http://localhost:8000/demo/` and you should see the same response that we got before we created the template file:

My favorite color is blue

Using template filters

If we want to modify the output of a variable, we can use a template filter. Filters modify the way a context variable is displayed in the output. As we saw earlier, they are applied using a pipe symbol directly after the variable. Do not put a space between the variable and the pipe.

To make the value of our `fav_color` variable be displayed entirely in capital letters, we can use the `upper` filter. In your `mycompany/templates/example.html` file, add the `upper` filter to the template `fav_color` template variable:

```
My favorite color is {{ fav_color|upper }}.
```

Browse to `http://localhost:8000/demo/` and you should see this output:

My favorite color is BLUE

Using template tags to perform logical tests

We've already seen how variable substitution takes place. So let's use a template tag to perform some simple logic to compare values.

We're going to use the `ifequal` tag to test if the `fav_color` context variable has the value `blue`. The tag uses this syntax: `{% fequal <argument1> <argument2> %}`

Change your `mycompany/templates/example.html` template file to look like this:

```
{% ifequal fav_color 'blue' %}
  My favorite color is {{ fav_color }}.
{% else %}
  My favorite color is not blue.
{% endifequal %}
```

Browse to `http://localhost:8000/demo/` and you should see this output:

My favorite color is blue.

We can also use template tags to perform looping logic. It is very common in a template to loop over a set of values and perform an action on each value. Let's add a second color to our context variable and use a `for` loop in our template to write them out.

First, in your `detail` view, change your `fav_color` variable to a list of colors by using Python list syntax:

```
def detail(request):
    c = Context({ 'fav_color': ['blue','green'] })
    t = loader.get_template('example.html')
    rendered_template = t.render(c)
    return HttpResponse(rendered_template)
```

We'll use the `for` and `endfor` tags to loop through the list of favorite colors. Notice that we are using a variable called `color` to hold the value for each iteration of the loop. In this example, `fav_color` is our list of `colors` from the Context, and color is the current value in the loop. Make sure you change the variable in the curly brackets to use `color`.

Replace the contents of your `mycompany/templates/example.html` file with these lines:

```
{% for color in fav_color %}
  My favorite color is {{ color }}.<br/>
{% endfor %}
```

The resulting output will look like this:

My favorite color is blue.

My favorite color is green.

Adding comments

If you want to add comments to your templates, you have two options: single-line and multi-line comments. If you want to make a comment that only spans a single line, you can wrap your comment with a curly bracket and hash (pound sign) syntax:

```
{% for color in fav_color %}
  {# We are writing out a comment here #}
  My favorite color is {{ color }}.<br/>
{% endfor %}
```

If you want to make comments that span multiple lines, you can wrap your comments in a `comment` tag. Note that the `comment` tag requires an ending `endcomment` tag:

```
{% comment %}
My comment
is more than
one line long
{% endcomment %}
```

Summary

That's it for our Django introduction and templating overview. Hopefully, you were able to follow along and got a taste for what we'll be covering in this book.

In this chapter, we:

- Discussed why templates are critical to development
- Explored how Django processes requests
- Covered the syntax of Django templates including filters, tags, and comments

We also set up a new Django project and configured it to run a test application. This project will be used throughout the book, so make sure you were able to get it working before continuing.

In the next chapter, we'll look at views and generic views to understand where templates get loaded and rendered.

2

Views, URLs, and Generic Views

Many developers new to Django get tripped up on the vocabulary and purpose of different pieces of the system—models, views, generic views, model managers, and so on. With some functions belonging to models and others to views, it can be confusing to know where to put the logic of your applications.

The view is where most of your application logic will be executed. Before we can work with views, however, we need to look at the URL dispatching system to see how a view is matched up with an incoming request. Once we have seen the URL dispatcher and some working views, we'll take a look at some shortcuts Django offers us to accomplish these actions even more quickly.

You can write entire Django sites without using models, but you'd have a hard time doing that without views or generic views.

In this chapter, we will:

- Create a sample application to work with
- Learn how the URL dispatcher works and how URLs are matched to views
- Explore the structure of views
- Build views to display a list of content and content detail
- See how to cut down development time with generic views
- Examine when to use regular views instead of generic views

An overview

Views are at the heart of Django and hold most of your application logic. They are nothing more than Python functions that take an HTTP request as input and return an HTTP response or error.

A mechanism called the dispatcher identifies an incoming URL against a set of URL patterns and their associated view functions. When a match is found, the associated view is called and the request gets handled.

Since many views follow a common strategy of loading an object or list, loading a template, rendering the template, and returning a response, Django offers a way of doing this without writing a view function. These *generic views* are called from the URL dispatcher and go right to the template.

Creating the application

Before we start looking at views and URLs, let's create a sample application to experiment with. Since most books and examples use blog models as their demos, let's keep things fresh by making our demo a press release application for a company website. The press release object will have a title, body, published date, and author name.

Create the data model

In the root directory of your project (in the directory `projects/mycompany`), create the press application by using the `startapp` command:

```
$ python manage.py startapp press
```

This will create a `press` folder in your site. Edit the `mycompany/press/models.py` file:

```
from django.db import models

class PressRelease(models.Model):
    title = models.CharField(max_length=100)
    body = models.TextField()
    pub_date = models.DateTimeField()
    author = models.CharField(max_length=100)

    def __unicode__(self):
        return self.title
```

Create the admin file

To take advantage of the automatic admin interface that Django gives us, we need to create a file called an `admin` file. Create a file called `admin.py` in the `mycompany/press` directory, adding these lines:

```
from django.contrib import admin
from mycompany.press.models import PressRelease

admin.site.register(PressRelease)
```

 If you've used Django before version 1.0, this step is new. The admin configuration directives were taken out of the model and put into their own files starting in version 1.0.

Add the `press` and `admin` applications to your `INSTALLED_APPS` variable in the `settings.py` file:

```
INSTALLED_APPS = (
    'django.contrib.auth',
    'django.contrib.admin',
    'django.contrib.contenttypes',
    'django.contrib.sessions',
    'django.contrib.sites',
    'mycompany.press',
)
```

In the root directory of your project, run the `syncdb` command to add the new models to the database:

```
$ python manage.py syncdb
```

Because we have Django's authentication system listed as one of our installed applications, the initial `syncdb` process will ask us if we want to create a superuser. Go ahead and create a superuser account; you will be using it later to access the admin site.

Configure the URLs

Finally, edit the `mycompany/urls.py` file:

```
from django.conf.urls.defaults import *
from django.contrib import admin

admin.autodiscover()

urlpatterns = patterns('',
    (r'^admin/(.*)', admin.site.root),
)
```

If you have completed Chapter 1, you probably have a URL pattern for the demo application that we used. You can remove it as we won't be using it again.

Add data in the admin application

By adding `django.contrib.admin` to our INSTALLED_APPS setting and creating a URL mapping for it, we can access the admin site by browsing to `http://localhost:8000/admin/`.

Go into the admin app and add two or three press releases so that we have some sample data to work with:

Mapping URLs to views

When Django accepts an incoming request, one of the first things it does is that it looks at the URL and tries to match it against a group of URL patterns. In order to identify patterns, Django uses regular expressions to see if the URLs follow a known format.

Consider these URLs:

```
http://localhost:8000/press/detail/1/
http://localhost:8000/press/detail/2/
```

These URLs appear to follow a pattern that they start with `press/detail/` and end with a number that represents the ID of a press release. (Recall that we don't work with the domain name portion of the URL. Django takes care of this automatically for us and just sends us everything that follows the domain name.)

With this pattern, we can add a new line to our `mycompany/urls.py` file:

```
from django.conf.urls.defaults import *
from django.contrib import admin

admin.autodiscover()

urlpatterns = patterns('',
    (r'^admin/(.*)', admin.site.root),
    (r'^press/detail/\d+/$', 'mycompany.press.views.detail'),
)
```

If you're not familiar with Python's regular expressions, this new line may look a bit wonky. This is the most important part:

```
r'^press/detail/\d+/$'
```

It reads like this: "A string that starts with `press/detail/` and ends with one or more digits followed by a slash".

The second segment of the new line is the view function that will get called when an incoming URL matches this pattern. In this case, it will be a function called `detail` in the `mycompany/press/views.py` file.

There's only one problem with this pattern—it recognizes that a number will be at the end of the URL, but doesn't do anything to pass that number to the view when it's called.

We can use a Python regular expression group to capture that number:

```
urlpatterns = patterns('',
    (r'^admin/', include('django.contrib.admin.urls')),
    (r'^press/detail/(?P<pid>\d+)/$',
        'mycompany.press.views.detail'),
)
```

This grouping syntax looks really funky, but it's easy to understand once you've seen it a few times. (?P) is the Python syntax for a *named group*, which allows the regular expression to save the piece that matched, and put a label on it so that we can call it later. The <pid> part is where we assign the label of pid to the ID of the press release that was sent with the URL.

In the case of this URL, the named group pid will be equal to 2:

```
http://localhost:8000/press/detail/2/
```

Any named groups that we get from a URL are passed as arguments to our view function. In this example, our detail function in press/views.py will have a method signature like this:

```
def detail(request, pid):
    p = PressRelease.object.get(id=pid)
    ...
```

There are two keyword arguments to the detail function, request and pid. (Django automatically passes the keyword request, which we'll explore a little later.)

Because we used a named group in the URL configuration to capture the press release ID, it's passed to our detail function as pid. You can use multiple named groups in your URL patterns to capture multiple pieces of information and pass them to your functions.

 Note: URL configurations and patterns are usually referred to as URLConf. You will see them named in this way in other parts of this book.

Handling unmatched URL patterns

URLs are matched up with view functions when they match patterns, but what happens when a match isn't found? This URL wouldn't match the patterns we created because it doesn't end in a number:

```
http://localhost:8000/press/detail/abc/
```

In this case, the URL dispatcher wouldn't match against our pattern and would keep trying other patterns until a match is found. If no match is found, a **404** error is raised. If you have debug set to true (**DEBUG=True**) in your settings file, you'll see an error message like this:

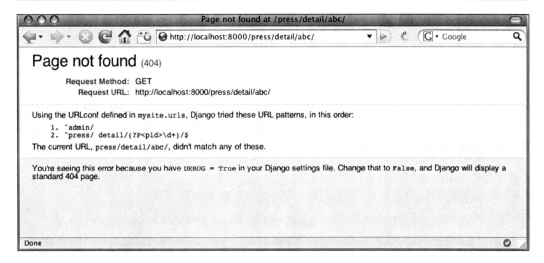

Splitting up the URL configurations

We created the URL configurations for the `press` application in the `mycompany/urls.py` file. While this is perfectly acceptable, sticking all the configurations into the main `urls.py` file can get unwieldy for large projects with many applications. It also isn't very modular if we want to share applications with others or use applications that other people distribute.

Instead of writing the press release configuration in our main `mycompany/urls.py` file, let's create a new file at `mycompany/press/urls.py`:

```
from django.conf.urls.defaults import *

urlpatterns = patterns('',
    (r'^detail/(?P<pid>\d+)/$', 'press.views.detail'),
)
```

This looks very similar to what we already have, but note that we've dropped `press` from the beginning of the regular expression. This line will match URLs that start with `detail`.

Open your `mycompany/urls.py` file and edit the highlighted line:

```
from django.conf.urls.defaults import *
from django.contrib import admin

admin.autodiscover()

urlpatterns = patterns('',
    (r'^admin/(.*)', admin.site.root),
    (r'^press/', include('mycompany.press.urls')),
)
```

We've changed the regular expression portion to match URLs that start with `press/`. If one is found, Django will hop over to the `press/urls.py` file to try to match the rest of the URL (without the `press/` prefix).

With this setup, we are telling Django that any URLs that start with `press` will be handled in a separate `urls.py` file in the `press` directory.

Creating views

Now that we're matching a URL to a view and passing it information, we can look at how a view is structured. Views have two rules you must follow:

1. The view must accept the `request` object as its first argument.
2. The view must return an HTTP response or an exception.

Beyond this, just remember that a view is a standard Python function and you can do just about anything in it that you can do in a Python program.

Accepting the request object

Our first rule for views states that a view must accept the `request` object as its first argument. What is this `request` object?

Django automatically creates the `request` object when a page is requested. It contains data about the incoming HTTP request such as the requestor's IP address, user agent, request method, cookies, GET parameters, POST parameters, and so on. Everything you should need to know about an incoming request will be found in this object.

When you build your view functions, always specify `request` as the first keyword argument:

```
def detail(request):
    # Python code here
```

If you forget to add `request` as the first parameter, you'll know quickly because your view will fail to load with some kind of error message about the arguments (the exact error depends on what other keyword arguments you might be using).

Responding with an HTTP response

The second rule for views is that a view must return an HTTP response or an exception. Let's start by talking about what an HTTP response is.

In order for a browser to understand how to render a web page, it looks at some special hidden information called **headers**, which is sent by the server along with the content or document being requested. These headers tell the browser information such as what kind of web server is sending the response, which version of the HTTP protocol is being used, how big the content is, and what kind of content is being sent.

Luckily, we don't have to worry about most of this because the web server and Django take care of it for us. All we have to do is make sure we send the response out of our view using the HttpResponse method.

In your mycompany/press/views.py file, add the following lines:

```
from django.http import HttpResponse

def detail(request, pid):
    return HttpResponse('This is just a test.')
```

Point your browser to http://localhost:8000/press/detail/1/. Here's what it should look like:

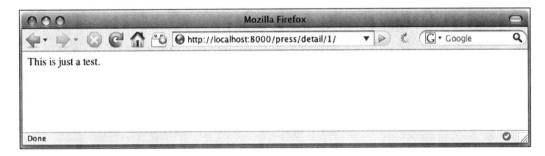

Obviously, our views are going to be more complicated than this one, but it illustrates how simple they can be.

Responding with an exception

The second part of our rule said that the view can respond with an exception instead of an HTTP response. When Django encounters an error during the processing of a view, we usually want to return a friendly error message to the user to let them know something went wrong (as opposed to just sending back a blank screen). Usually, these error messages are in the form of 404 or 500 Error pages.

404 errors are also known as *page not found* errors. Anyone who has spent time surfing the Web has undoubtedly encountered a 404 Error page when clicking an old link that is no longer valid. In traditional HTML publishing, 404 errors popped up when the user requested a filename that wasn't found on the server (that's where the "page" in "page not found" comes from). With Django, we don't have URLs that represent filenames on the server, but we still return a 404 error when the user is looking for a resource that does not exist.

Django makes it easy to return a 404 page by returning the error using the `HttpResponseNotFound` function:

```
from django.http import HttpResponseNotFound

def detail(request, pid):
    return HttpResponseNotFound('Page Not Found')
```

Similarly, requests that cause errors on the server are usually referred to as 500 errors. (500 is the standard HTTP response code for a server error.) Django also makes it easy to serve a 500 error:

```
from django.http import HttpResponseServerError

def detail(request, pid):
    return HttpResponseServerError('An Error Has Occurred.')
```

Putting the views together

Now that we know how a view works and what it needs to do, let's write the real view to work with our sample application.

Building the basic view

In your `mycompany/press/views.py` file, replace any contents with the following lines:

```
from django.http import HttpResponse
from django.http import HttpResponseNotFound
from mycompany.press.models import PressRelease

def detail(request, pid):
    '''
    Accepts a press release ID and returns the detail page
    '''
    try:
        p = PressRelease.objects.get(id=pid)
        return HttpResponse(p.title)
    except PressRelease.DoesNotExist:
        return HttpResponseNotFound('Press Release Not Found')
```

If you'd like to test it out, point your browser to `http://localhost:8000/press/ detail/1/`. You should see the title of your press release. Change the number at the end of the press release to an ID that doesn't exist (such as 99) and you should get a **Page Not Found** error.

This view doesn't return a very pretty output, but it follows the rule that the view must serve an HTTP response or an error/exception. The `try/except` error handling to make sure the press release exists is kind of ugly. Luckily, Django gives us a more elegant way of handling it.

Cleaning up the error handling

Instead of putting a `try/except` block around the object lookup, Django has a `get_object_or_404` method that will automatically raise an error if the object is not found.

Change the highlighted lines in your `mycompany/press/views.py` file:

```
from django.http import HttpResponse
from django.shortcuts import get_object_or_404
from mycompany.press.models import PressRelease

def detail(request, pid):
    '''
    Accepts a press release ID and returns the detail page
    '''
    p = get_object_or_404(PressRelease, id=pid)
    return HttpResponse(p.title)
```

That's a much cleaner way of doing things!

 Note: If you're getting a list instead of an object, Django has a `get_list_ or_404` method that you can use. We'll see this in a few pages.

Adding the template files

The last thing we need to do is add a way to load up the response with the output of a rendered template. All of this syntax will be covered in detail in a later chapter; don't worry if you don't completely understand everything you see yet.

We're going to load a template file, replace placeholders in that file with our data (called "rendering" the template), and then return the contents of the template as a string as an HTTP response.

In the first chapter, we created a `templates` directory at `mycompany/templates`, and configured the `settings.py` file to tell Django where to find it:

```
TEMPLATE_DIRS = (
    '/projects/mycompany/templates/',
)
```

Verify that you have configured your project this way before continuing. With this setting in place, we can load templates relative to this path.

Create a directory under the `mycompany/templates` directory called `press`. (It's common practice to use subdirectories to group template files by the application they are associated with.)

Create a new file at `mycompany/templates/press/detail.html` and add these lines:

```
<html>
<head>
<title>{{ press.title }}</title>
</head>
<body>
<h1>{{ press.title }}</h1>
<p>
Author: {{ press.author }}<br/>
Date: {{ press.pub_date }}<br/>
</p>
<p>
{{ press.body }}
</p>
</body>
</html>
```

This simple template file has placeholders for our `title`, `author`, `pub_date`, and `body` fields. When the template is rendered, these placeholders will be replaced with their respective values.

Now that we have a template, we can tell the view to use it.

Adding the template to the view

In our `mycompany/press/views.py` file, let's add a few lines to load our template. Replace the contents of your file with these lines:

```
from django.http import HttpResponse
from django.shortcuts import get_object_or_404
from django.template import loader, Context
from mycompany.press.models import PressRelease

def detail(request, pid):
    '''
    Accepts a press release ID and returns the detail page
    '''
    p = get_object_or_404(PressRelease, id=1)
    t = loader.get_template('press/detail.html')
    c = Context({'press': p})
    rendered_template = t.render(c)
    return HttpResponse(rendered_template)
```

In the function, we're retrieving the `press/detail.html` template file and creating a special data object called `Context`. We'll cover the `Context` object in great detail in a later chapter. So for now, just understand that it passes data to the template so that it can be rendered. The context object in this example passes our press release object to the template in a variable called `press`.

Our template gets rendered into a string called `rendered_template` that is sent back to the browser via `HttpResponse` the same way we sent back simple lines of text in previous examples.

The `rendered_template` variable was used for clarity. You can omit it and just return the response like this:

```
def detail(request, pid):
    '''
    Accepts a press release ID and returns the detail page
    '''
    p = get_object_or_404(PressRelease, id=1)
    t = loader.get_template('press/detail.html')
    c = Context({'press': p})
    return HttpResponse(t.render(c))
```

Point your browser to the URL `http://localhost:8000/detail/1/`. You should see something like this depending on what you entered earlier into the admin site as sample data:

Creating the list view and template

In addition to displaying the detail for a specific press release, we'll also need a way to display a list of press releases. The steps to add this will be very similar to what we just did to add our detail view.

In your `mycompany/press/views.py` file, add the highlighted lines:

```
from django.http import HttpResponse
from django.shortcuts import get_object_or_404
from django.shortcuts import get_list_or_404
from django.template import loader, Context
from mycompany.press.models import PressRelease

def detail(request, pid):
    '''
    Accepts a press release ID and returns the detail page
    '''
    p = get_object_or_404(PressRelease, id=1)
    t = loader.get_template('press/detail.html')
    c = Context({'press': p})
    return HttpResponse(t.render(c))

def press_list(request):
    '''
    Returns a list of press releases
    '''
    pl = get_list_or_404(PressRelease)
    t = loader.get_template('press/list.html')
    c = Context({'press_list': pl})
    return HttpResponse(t.render(c))
```

In your `mycompany/press/urls.py` file, add the highlighted line:

```
from django.conf.urls.defaults import *

urlpatterns = patterns('',
    (r'detail/(?P<pid>\d+)/$','mycompany.press.views.detail'),
    (r'list/$', 'mycompany.press.views.press_list'),
)
```

Any incoming request starting with `press/` will be sent to our `press/urls.py` file. If the remaining part of the URL is `list/`, it will be handled by the `press_list` function in our `press/views.py` file. If the remaining part is `detail/<number>` (such as `detail/1` or `detail/2`), it will be handled by the `detail` function.

Finally, create a new file at `mycompany/templates/press/list.html`:

```html
<html>
<head>
<title>Press Releases</title>
</head>
<body>
<h1>Press Releases</h1>
<ul>
{% for press in press_list %}
<li>
<a href="/press/detail/{{ press.id }}/">
{{ press.title }}</a>
</li>
{% endfor %}
</ul>
</body>
</html>
```

Point your browser to the URL `http://localhost:8000/press/list/`. You should see something like this, depending on what you entered earlier into the admin site:

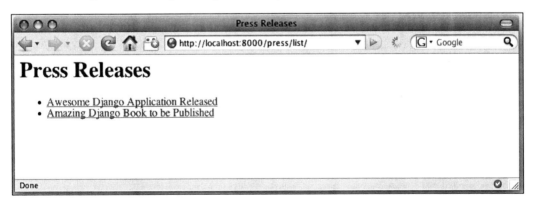

Using generic views to shorten development time

What we've done so far in this chapter is pretty standard for web
application development:

- We created a view to load an object by its ID.
- We created a view to load a list of objects.
- We retrieved our object using the data sent in from the URL or retrieved a list of objects.
- We loaded a template file.
- We rendered the template.
- We returned an HTTP response.

Because these actions are so common, Django has a way to cut out the whole step
of writing a view, called **generic views**. Generic views are called from the URL
configuration file, which allows you to go right from the URL pattern to
your template.

Generic views come in a few types:

- Simple
- List/detail
- Date-based
- Create/update/delete

We won't be covering the date-based or create/update/delete generic views.
But after reading this chapter, you'll be well-prepared to read about them in the
online documentation.

Simple generic views

The two simple generic views that handle loading of a template don't require any
data lookup (going directly to a template) and redirecting from one URL to another.

Loading a template directly

If you just need to load and render a template when a URL is requested, you can use
the `direct_to_template` generic view.

For example, let's build a robots exclusion file (aka a `robots.txt` file) that search
engine spiders will request at `http://localhost:8000/robots.txt`. (Search
engines wouldn't index pages on a localhost domain, but pretend for this example
that they would.)

Since the file is rarely changed after being created, you may not want the overhead of a database lookup to serve it, so you just want to render a template when the URL is requested.

Create a new file at `mycompany/templates/robots.txt` and add these lines:

```
User-agent: *
Disallow: /admin
```

This very simple example will prevent spiders from trying to index your admin path (visit `robotstxt.org` for more info on how exclusion files work).

In your `mycompany/urls.py` file, add the highlighted lines:

```
from django.conf.urls.defaults import *
from django.contrib import admin

admin.autodiscover()

urlpatterns = patterns('',
    (r'^admin/(.*)', admin.site.root),
    (r'^press/', include('mycompany.press.urls')),
    (r'^robots.txt$',
        'django.views.generic.simple.direct_to_template',
        'template': 'robots.txt'}),
    )
```

Point your browser to the URL `http://localhost:8000/robots.txt/`. You'll get a response that looks like this:

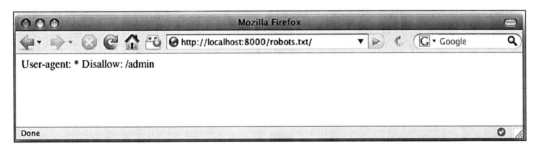

Redirecting URLs

If you want to automatically redirect one URL to another, you can use the `redirect_to` generic view.

For example, you might want to redirect from `http://localhost:8000/press/` to `http://localhost:8000/press/list/`.

In your `mycompany/press/urls.py` file, add the highlighted line:

```
from django.conf.urls.defaults import *

urlpatterns = patterns('',
    (r'detail/(?P<pid>\d+)/$','mycompany.press.views.detail'),
    (r'list/$', 'mycompany.press.views.press_list'),
    (r'$', 'django.views.generic.simple.redirect_to',
        {'url': '/press/list/'})
)
```

Point your browser to the URL `http://localhost:8000/press/` and you will be redirected to `http://localhost:8000/press/list/`.

List/detail generic views

Generic views that handle object lists and object details can speed up your development time. Instead of writing views that do routine logic of retrieving object(s), loading and rendering templates, and then returning a response, we let the generic views do the heavy lifting for us.

Replacing the list view

Consider the `press_list` view we built earlier in the chapter at `mycompany/press/views.py`:

```
def press_list(request):
    '''
    Returns a list of press releases
    '''
    pl = get_list_or_404(PressRelease)
    t = loader.get_template('press/list.html')
    c = Context({'press_list': pl})
    return HttpResponse(t.render(c))
```

We can completely replace the logic of this view by replacing our `list` configuration with a generic view.

Replace the highlighted lines in the `mycompany/press/urls.py` file:

```
from django.conf.urls.defaults import *
from mycompany.press.models import PressRelease

press_list_dict = {
    'queryset': PressRelease.objects.all(),
```

```
    }

urlpatterns = patterns('',
    (r'detail/(?P<pid>\d+)/$','mycompany.press.views.detail'),
    (r'list/$',
        'django.views.generic.list_detail.object_list',
        press_list_dict),
    (r'$', 'django.views.generic.simple.redirect_to',
        {'url': '/press/list/'})
)
```

When you use generic views, some default assumptions will be made. For our example, we need to worry about these defaults:

- The list of objects you send to the template in the context will be called `object_list` — this is a problem for us because our list of objects is called `press_list`.

- It's OK to send an empty list to the template — currently, our view returns a **404 Error** if the list is empty.

- The template file will be called `appname/modelname_list.html` — currently, our template is called `press/list.html`.

We are faced with two choices: change our code or override these defaults. It would be easy to change our view and template name, but instead let's override the defaults by adding some extra keys to the dictionary we pass to the generic view.

Add the highlighted lines to the `mycompany/press/urls.py` file:

```
press_list_dict = {
    'queryset': PressRelease.objects.all(),
    'template_name': 'press/list.html',
    'allow_empty': False,
    'template_object_name': 'press',
}
```

By passing these overrides, we make our templates work as we created them.

You may be wondering about the value of the last key, `template_object_name`. Why is its value `press` when we are looking for an object named `press_list` in our template? Generic views add `_list` to the object name, so to get an object named `press_list`, we pass a `template_object_name` of `press`.

Replacing the detail view

Consider the `detail` view we created earlier in `mycompany/press/views.py`:

```
from django.http import HttpResponse
from django.shortcuts import get_object_or_404
from django.shortcuts import get_list_or_404
from django.template import loader, Context
from mycompany.press.models import PressRelease

def detail(request, pid):
    '''
    Accepts a press release ID and returns the detail page
    '''
    p = get_object_or_404(PressRelease, id=1)
    t = loader.get_template('press/detail.html')
    c = Context({'press': p})
    return HttpResponse(t.render(c))
```

Just as we did with the list view, we can replace the logic of this detail view by replacing our "detail" configuration with a generic view.

Add the highlighted lines to the `mycompany/press/urls.py` file:

```
from django.conf.urls.defaults import *
from mycompany.press.models import PressRelease

press_detail_dict={
    'queryset': PressRelease.objects.all(),
    'template_name': 'press/detail.html',
    'template_object_name': 'press',
}

press_list_dict={
    'queryset': PressRelease.objects.all(),
    'template_name': 'press/list.html',
    'allow_empty': False,
    'template_object_name': 'press',
}

urlpatterns=patterns('',
    (r'detail/(?P<object_id>\d+)/$',
        'django.views.generic.list_detail.object_detail',
        press_detail_dict),
    (r'list/$',
```

```
            'django.views.generic.list_detail.object_list',
             press_list_dict),
       (r'$', 'django.views.generic.simple.redirect_to',
           {'url': '/press/list/'})
   )
```

A couple of things to note are:

- We changed the name of the press release ID captured in the URL from `pid` to `object_id`. Generic views expect a variable called `object_id` and though there are ways to get around it, it's much simpler to change the name to what Django is expecting.

- Looking at the `press_detail_dict` dictionary, it looks as if we are retrieving all of the press releases in our queryset, but the generic view is automatically going to use the `object_id` from our URL to filter the appropriate object.

- There is no `allow_empty` key in the `press_detail_dict`. If the generic view can't find the object, it automatically returns a 404 error.

We have now completely replaced the functionality of the view functions in `mycompany/press/views.py`.

Using the other generic views

As mentioned, generic views come in two other varieties, date-based and create/update/delete. We won't be covering them, but here's a quick summary to whet your appetite for further exploration.

Date-based generic views allow you to create archives for your models that have a `DateField` or `DateTimeField`. You can set up different views for yearly, monthly, weekly, and daily displays of your content.

Create/update/delete generic views allow you to set up form-based pages to add new content, edit content, and delete content from your models. They are very similar to the add/edit pages from the admin application, and perform the same validation.

Comparing views and generic views

Now that we've seen both views and the generic views, you may be wondering why you would choose to use one over the other. The answer is usually found in the complexity of what you are trying to accomplish.

Don't let the simplicity of generic views fool you; entire sites have been written with only generic views. They can be much more complex than our simple examples were in this chapter, taking many additional arguments for specific functionality.

Try to use generic views when you can, and fall back to regular views when the complexity exceeds what you feel comfortable trying to do in a generic view. You may discover that what you want to do can be accomplished in a generic view, but that it's much simpler to do the same with a regular view.

Summary

In this chapter we learned how views and generic views can be used to display content. We explored how the URL dispatcher works and how it matches URLs to their associated view functions. We also learned how to pass data from the URL into our views using regular expressions. We built views to show a list of content and a content detail page, and then used generic views to reproduce that functionality.

In the next chapter, we will look at the Context, the object that makes variables from our view available to the template during rendering.

3
Template Context

The Context is a special collection of data that is used to pass information from your views into your templates. Since the template system is only allowed to work with values that you explicitly give it access to, understanding how to work with the Context is a very important skill for template design and debugging.

In this chapter, we will:

- Learn how the `Context` object works
- Work with context values in templates
- Explore some shortcuts for rendering the context
- Use context processors to automatically add values to the context
- Use Django shortcuts to simplify rendering a template in context

The context explained

As we have seen earlier, the Context is a mapping of variable names to values. When the template is rendered, these values are made available to the template engine and fill in "the holes" in your templates by replacing variables with their respective values.

Technically, the Context is a class in Django that we instantiate before rendering a template. A context is a mapping of a single variable name to a value. When we render the template, we are usually registering multiple contexts, or multiple mappings of variable names to values. Don't get hung up on the semantics. When we're talking about context, just think about the variables that are made available to the template.

To use the Context, we import the `Context` class from `django.template.Context`. When we instantiate it, we can pass a dictionary of variable names as an optional argument.

To experiment with the Context, we can launch the Django interactive shell by running these commands:

```
$ cd /projects/mycompany
$ python manage.py shell
```

This command launches the Django shell that allows you to interactively work with the Python code and Django libraries. By using the shell, we can experiment with the template without having to create a whole view, run the development server, and load the URL in a browser. Here's an example:

```
>>> from django.template import Context, Template
>>> c = Context({'fav_color': 'blue'})
>>> print c
[{'fav_color': 'blue'}]
```

 When using the Django shell, each line begins with >>>, which is sometimes called **chevrons**. Anything output from the shell (such as a print statement), will not have the chevrons at the beginning of the line.

When the template is rendered, the template variable is replaced with the corresponding item from the context. We can simulate that here by creating a string with a variable to be substituted, then running the `render` method on it:

```
>>> from django.template import Context, Template
>>> c = Context({'fav_color': 'blue'})
>>> t = Template('My favorite color is {{ fav_color }}.')
>>> print t.render(c)
My favorite color is blue.
```

Recall that a template is just a string of text characters and can be either loaded from a file or passed to the `Template` object as a string.

Though the Context is a class, it behaves like a dictionary. You can use the standard Python dictionary syntax methods such as `pop()`, `push()`, `get()`, `has_keys()` and `update()`. You can remove keys and add new ones.

Practicing working with the context

Understanding the context object is an important skill when working with templates, so let's get some practice with it in an actual Django view. We'll add a new page to our press release application that we started in Chapter 2, which shows information about the most recent press release.

In your `mycompany/press/models.py` file, add the highlighted lines:

```
class PressRelease(models.Model):
    title = models.CharField(max_length=100)
    body = models.TextField()
    pub_date = models.DateTimeField()
    author = models.CharField(max_length=100)

    class Meta:
        get_latest_by = 'pub_date'

    def get_absolute_url(self):
        return '/press/detail/%d/' % self.id

    def __unicode__(self):
        return self.title
```

These highlighted lines tell Django that when we're trying to look up the latest record, use `pub_date` to find the record with the most recent date. It also gives us a way to return a hyperlink to the press release detail view by adding a function to the class called `get_absolute_url`.

In your `mycompany/press/views.py` file, add the following view function to the end of the file:

```
def latest(request):
    ''' Returns information on the latest press release '''
    p = PressRelease.objects.latest()
    t = loader.get_template('press/latest.html')
    c = Context({
        'title': p.title,
        'author': p.author,
        'date': p.pub_date,
        'link': p.get_absolute_url(),
    })
    return HttpResponse(t.render(c))
```

In your `mycompany/press/urls.py` file, add the highlighted line to the `patterns` declaration:

```
urlpatterns = patterns('',
    (r'detail/(?P<object_id>\d+)/$',
        'django.views.generic.list_detail.object_detail',
        press_detail_dict),
    (r'list/$',
        'django.views.generic.list_detail.object_list',
        press_list_dict),
    (r'latest/$', 'mycompany.press.views.latest'),
    (r'$', 'django.views.generic.simple.redirect_to',
        {'url': '/press/list/'})
)
```

Finally, create a new template called `latest.html` in the `mycompany/templates/press/` directory with the following lines:

```
<html>
<head>
<title>Latest Press Release</title>
</head>
<body>
<h1>{{ title }}</h1>
<p>
Author: {{ author }}<br/>
Date: {{ date }}<br/>
<a href="{{ link }}">View Detail</a><br/>
</p>
</body>
</html>
```

Point your browser to the URL `http://localhost:8000/press/latest/`. You'll see something like this (depending on the value of your latest press release):

What we've done is pretty common when working with an existing project and application. We have:

- Added a new view function.
- Added a new template.
- Edited the existing model to add functionality.
- Added a new template file.
- Added a new URL mapping to point to our view function.

This was a lot of work just to create a way for us to practice the template context, but it's a great practice for working in Django.

In `mycompany/press/views.py` file, consider the highlighted lines:

```
def latest(request):
    ''' Returns information on the latest press release '''
    p = PressRelease.objects.latest()
    t = loader.get_template('press/latest.html')
    c = Context({
        'title': p.title,
        'author': p.author,
        'date': p.pub_date,
        'link': p.get_absolute_url(),
    })
    return HttpResponse(t.render(c))
```

These lines explicitly pass the variables `title`, `author`, `date`, and `link` to the template Context object. When the template engine renders the template file, it relies on the Context to find the appropriate values to replace the template variables with.

> We could have simply passed the variable p to and looked up the properties from within the template. But we did this to illustrate the concept of passing values to the Context object (we'll clean this up later in the chapter).

Using locals for prototyping

It can sometimes feel redundant to list all your variables when instantiating your `Context` variable. If you don't want to explicitly pass them, you can use a Python built-in function called `locals()` that returns a dictionary of all the variables defined in the current function.

In our previous example, we could have used `locals()` to pass variables to the Context:

```
def latest(request):
    ''' Returns information on the latest press release '''
    p = PressRelease.objects.latest()
    title = p.title
    author = p.author
    date = p.pub_date
    link = p.get_absolute_url()
    t = loader.get_template('press/latest.html')
    c = Context(locals())
    return HttpResponse(t.render(c))
```

This didn't save us any code, but it illustrates the point about passing all the variables defined in the function. One thing to notice about this example is that the variable p will also be passed to the template because it has been defined in the function.

> Using `locals()` is good for quick testing and prototyping, but you will probably want to explicitly choose the variables that are passed to the Context. This can help make your code more efficient and maintainable in the long run.
>
> In complex views, there may be values you don't want to be available to the template. Or, you may want to use different variable names in the view than you do in your template for readability. Explicitly passing your Context values can help in both these situations.

Adding, changing, and removing items in the context

There may be times you want to change the context after you have instantiated it. This isn't that common in a view, since assigning context mappings is one of the last things we do before rendering the template. But the context might even be manipulated from within a template tag.

Django's `regroup` tag, for example, does this. When you run it against a list of objects, the tag creates a new, grouped list in the current context that is then available to the rest of your template.

You can also create your own custom tags that are able to change the context. We'll save that for the chapter on template tags, but for now just remember that you can add, edit, and remove context items with the standard Python dictionary syntax.

Here's an example using the Django shell that demonstrates how to do this:

```
>>> # Create an empty context object
>>> c = Context()
>>>
>>> # Add a value to the context
>>> c['fav_color'] = 'blue'
>>> print c
[{'fav_color': 'blue'}]
>>>
>>> # Add a new item to the context
>>> c['new_fav'] = 'red'
>>> print c
[{'new_fav': 'red', 'fav_color': 'blue'}]
>>>
>>> # Remove an item from the context
>>> del(c['fav_color'])
>>> print c
[{'new_fav': 'red'}]
>>>
>>> # Change the value of an existing item
>>> c['new_fav'] = 'orange'
>>> print c
[{'new_fav': 'orange'}]
>>>
>>> # See if an item exists
>>> c.has_key('new_fav')
True
```

Using the context values in your templates

We worked with template variables in the first chapter, but didn't discuss some of the subtleties of working with different kinds of data such as methods, objects, lists, and dictionaries. The template engine provides us with a simple way to work with different kinds of data by consistently using a dotted syntax. Regardless of the type of data you are trying to retrieve, you use the same syntax.

Let's look at some examples using the Django shell to keep things simple. We'll pass strings to the Template object again to keep the examples clear, instead of loading the text from template files.

Note: If you are not familiar with Python dictionaries, lists, objects, and methods, you'll probably want to brush up on these concepts before going any further. If you don't understand what you are putting into a template, you won't understand what you're getting back out.

A great reference is Mark Pilgrim's *Dive Into Python*, available for free at diveintopython.org.

The most basic example is using a plain old variable in your template:

```
>>> # Create a simple variable string
>>> favorite = 'blue'
>>> c = Context({ 'favorite': favorite })
>>> t = Template("My favorite color is {{ favorite }}.")
>>> print t.render(c)
My favorite color is blue.
```

This example was pretty simple. We created a string, put it in the context, and then referenced it from the template.

If you want to use a dictionary, you access the keys with dotted notation:

```
>>> # Create an empty dictionary
>>> favorite = {}
>>> favorite['color'] = 'blue'
>>> c = Context({ 'favorite': favorite })
>>> t = Template('My favorite color is {{ favorite.color }}.')
>>> print t.render(c)
My favorite color is blue.
```

In this example, we created a dictionary and assigned it a key called color with a value of blue. From the template, we are able to access the key by referring to the dictionary's key using a dotted syntax. (Normally in Python, you'd use brackets to refer to a dictionary's key.)

If you want to access the property of an object, you also use a dotted notation:

```
>>> # Create an empty Object
>>> class Favorite():
>>>     pass
>>>
>>> # Instantiate the object
>>> favorite = Favorite()
>>>
>>> # Assign an arbitrary property to the object
>>> favorite.color = 'blue'
```

```
>>>
>>> c = Context({ 'favorite': favorite })
>>> t = Template("My favorite color is {{ favorite.color }}.")
>>> print t.render(c)
My favorite color is blue.
```

In this example, we created an empty object and then assigned it a property called `color` with a value of `blue`. From the template, we are (again) able to get the value of the object using dotted syntax. This is one of the most common techniques we'll use in templates, since database records are returned as objects and the field values are available as properties of the object.

If you want to call a method of a class, you use dotted notation, but not parentheses or arguments:

```
>>> # Create a class with a single method
>>> class Favorite():
>>>     def get_color(self):
>>>         return 'blue'
>>>
>>> favorite = Favorite()
>>> c = Context({'favorite': favorite })
>>> t = Template('My favorite color is {{ favorite.get_color }}.')
>>> print t.render(c)
My favorite color is blue.
```

Here we are calling the `get_color` method of the `favorite` object from within the template. This example is important; the syntax of calling methods and functions trips up many beginners to Django templating.

The Django template system allows you to call methods, but you don't use parentheses as you would in the regular Python programming. Because you don't use parentheses, you cannot call methods that require arguments. This is done intentionally to keep programming logic out of the templates and to keep the template syntax simple.

Finally, if you want to access the value of a list element, you can refer to the index with dotted notation:

```
>>> color_list = ['orange', 'blue', 'green', 'red']
>>> c = Context({ 'favorite_colors': color_list })
>>> t = Template("My favorite color is {{ favorite_colors.0 }}.")
>>> print t.render(c)
My favorite color is orange.
```

Accessing a specific element of a list by index is not a common thing to do in your templates, but you should be aware that it can be done. This is a dangerous way to get the value, because if the list coming from your view is empty, the template will raise an exception and the page will not render.

Preventing method execution from templates

If you want to prevent a method from being called by a template, you can add an `alters_data` attribute to your function and set its value to `True`:

```
>>> class Account():
>>>     def wipeout(self):
>>>         self.bank_account.delete()
>>>         return "You are broke"
>>>     wipeout.alters_data = True
>>>
>>> account = Acccount()
>>> c = Context({"account": account})
>>> t = Template("Deleting Account: {{ account.wipeout }}.")
>>> print t.render(c)
Deleting Account: .
```

Though we tried executing the `wipeout()` method from inside the template, `alters_data` was `True`, and so the template engine prevented it from being called. (No errors are raised.)

By default, Django models apply `alters_data` to the `save()` and `delete()` methods of the model object and so they cannot be executed from inside a template. If you really wanted to be able to do this from your template (warning flags should be going off in your head if you do), you'll have to write your own custom template tag to do it.

Handling invalid context variables

Django has a handy way of handling references to invalid variables in your context—it does nothing! OK, that's not technically true, but you generally won't see any errors from your templates as a result of trying to use variables that don't exist.

If the variable does not exist, it is interpreted as an empty string (`' '`) or `None`, depending on what is trying to use it. If it's being called by the tags `if`, `for`, or `regroup`, the invalid variable will be treated as the value `None`. Anything else will treat it as an empty string because of the setting `TEMPLATE_STRING_IF_INVALID`.

By default, `TEMPLATE_STRING_IF_INVALID` is set to "" (empty string), so that is what is used in place of a value. For example:

```
>>> t = Template('Hello, my name is {{ bogus_variable }}.')
>>> t.render(c)
Hello, my name is .
```

If you set `TEMPLATE_STRING_IF_INVALID` to something else, the text you used will be rendered in place of the invalid variable.

 The Django documentation warns about changing `TEMPLATE_STRING_TO_INVALID` for anything except debugging because the Django admin app relies on this setting to be an empty string. You should really leave it as is!

The take-away from this is to understand that your site won't come to a screeching halt if it encounters an invalid variable, but you'll have to watch for silent variable failure.

Cleaning up the view

Earlier in the chapter, we experimented with our view called `latest` in the press application to populate the context using a few different techniques. Now that we are more familiar with Django template syntax, let's clean up the function to use best practices.

In your `mycompany/press/views.py` file, edit the `latest` function to look like this:

```
def latest(request):
    ''' Returns information on the latest press release '''
    p = PressRelease.objects.latest()
    t = loader.get_template('press/latest.html')
    c = Context({
        'press': p,
    })
    return HttpResponse(t.render(c))
```

In your `mycompany/templates/press/latest.html` file, edit the highlighted lines to look like this:

```
<html>
<head>
<title>Latest Press Release</title>
</head>
<body>
<h1>{{ press.title }}</h1>
```

```
<p>
Author: {{ press.author }}<br/>
Date: {{ press.pub_date }}<br/>
<a href="{{ press.get_absolute_url }}">View Detail</a><br/>
</p>
</body>
</html>
```

In the view function, we are passing an object p to our Context, and the context will pass it to the template as a variable called press. Instead of passing individual values to the template for title, author, date, and link, we pass the object press and allow the template to get its values from the object's properties. We changed the template file to look for the properties of the press object, instead of the individual variables it was using before.

Notice that we are also calling the function get_absolute_url from within the template and that it is called without parentheses.

Context rendering shortcuts

Django makes a few shortcuts available to save us from repetitive, common coding.

Using render_to_response()

Since it's pretty common to create a context, load a template, render the template, and then return the rendered string as an HTTP response, Django provides a shortcut at django.shortcuts.render_to_response to do this quickly.

In your mycompany/press/views.py file, add this line to the top of the file to import the render_to_response function:

```
from django.shortcuts import render_to_response
```

In the same file, edit the latest function to look like this:

```
def latest(request):
    ''' Returns information on the latest press release '''
    p = PressRelease.objects.latest()
    return render_to_response('press/latest.html', {
        'press': p,
    })
```

Instead of loading a template file, creating a context, and rendering the template with the context, we simply use the render_to_response function that takes a template as its first argument and context as its second to streamline the process.

Using render_to_string()

In addition to `render_to_response`, Django also provides a shortcut at `django.shortcuts.render_to_string` to render the template and context into a string instead of an HTTP response. This isn't terribly useful in the examples we've looked at here, but it's very useful when used in conjunction with the low-level caching API.

When using the low-level caching API, we take the rendered template string and cache the value before returning the HTTP response. The next visitor can get served the rendered template string from cache without having to perform all the logic in the view again.

We'll be working with Django caching in chapter 10.

Context processors

In the course of your Django development you may have data that you want to make available to your Context without having to specify it in every view. This could be things such as information about the current authenticated user, media settings, or a custom piece of data that you need in all of your templates. If you find yourself adding the same items to your Context in many views, it's a good candidate for a **context processor**.

Exploring the default context processors

Django provides us a set of libraries for commonly used context processors. These include `auth`, `debug`, `i18n`, and `media`. Each of these libraries adds extra variables to our context that we can use from within our templates.

Auth

`Auth` adds the variables `user`, `messages`, and `perms` to the context. `user` is the currently logged in user, `messages` is a list of messages for that user (you see this a lot in the admin app when you change something—it's the message at the top of the screen after you add/save/delete), and `perms` are the user's permissions. `perms` follows the format `perms.<application name>.<permission name>`.

Here is some example usage of these values in a template:

```
The current user is {{ user.username }}.
{% if messages %}
  {% for message in messages %}
    {{ message }}
  {% endfor %}
```

```
{% endif %}
{% if perms.press.can_add %}
  <a href='/press/post/'>Add a press release</a>
{% endif%}
```

Adding the `auth` context processor automatically added some `user`, `messages`, and `perms` values to our template.

Debug

Debug adds a Boolean variable `debug` to the context and a list called `sql_queries` that contains all the SQL queries run up to this point and their execution time. When using the `debug` processor, you can access these values from within your templates like this:

```
{% if debug %}
    {% for query in sql_queries %}
       <p>This query took {{ query.time }} seconds: {{ query.sql }}</p>
    {% endfor %}
{% endif %}
```

 The `debug` context processor requires two specific configurations in your `settings.py` file: debug must be set to `True`, and your computer's IP address must be in the `INTERNAL_IPS` list.

Media

Media adds a `MEDIA_URL` variable that has the value of your `MEDIA_URL` setting from the `settings.py` file. You can use `MEDIA_URL` in your templates so that you don't have to hard-code the address in your template:

```
<img src='{{ MEDIA_URL }}{{ press.image }}'/>
```

For this example, if `press.image` is equal to `press1.gif` and `MEDIA_URL` is `http://localhost:8000/media/`, this would get rendered in your template as:

```
<img src='http://localhost:8000/media/press1.gif'>
```

Using `MEDIA_URL` makes it easy to maintain your site if you need to change your link to your media location later.

i18n

The `i18n` processor deals with internationalization and gives you the ability to serve the same template in multiple languages. This is such a big topic that we'll be spending all of chapter 11 on it.

Configuring your project to use context processors

Now that we understand what the default context processors can do for us, we need to configure our project to use them. The first thing we need to do is add a new setting to our `mycompany/settings.py` file. Add this block of text anywhere in the file:

```
TEMPLATE_CONTEXT_PROCESSORS = (
    'django.core.context_processors.auth',
    'django.core.context_processors.debug',
    'django.core.context_processors.i18n',
    'django.core.context_processors.media',
)
```

While you are still in `mycompany/settings.py` file, change the value of `MEDIA_URL` to something other than the default empty string:

```
MEDIA_URL = 'http://localhost:8000/'
```

These settings make the four default context processors available to our views, but we need to make a slight change to our views before we can use them.

Configuring your views to use context processors

Before we can use our newly added context processors, we need to change our views to use a special version of the Context called `RequestContext`. Let's demonstrate this by using one of the views from Chapter 2.

Instead of calling the Context from our view like this:

```
def detail(request, pid):
    '''
    Accepts a press release ID and returns the detail page
    '''
    p = get_object_or_404(PressRelease, id=1)
    t = loader.get_template('press/detail.html')
    c = Context({'press': p})
    return HttpResponse(t.render(c))
```

we are going to import and use `RequestContext`:

```
from django.template import RequestContext

def detail(request, pid):
    '''
    Accepts a press release ID and returns the detail page
    '''
    p = get_object_or_404(PressRelease, id=1)
    t = loader.get_template('press/detail.html')
    c = RequestContext(request, {'press': p})
    return HttpResponse(t.render(c))
```

 Notice that the first argument to `RequestContext()` is a request object. Forgetting to include this is a common mistake!

You might be wondering what the `RequestContext` is and how it's different from the regular `Context` object we've been using so far. `RequestContext` works just like the regular `Context` object, but it requires the current request to be passed to it as an argument and adds some extra values to our Context.

The extra values it adds to the Context depend on what you are using in the `TEMPLATE_CONTEXT_PROCESSORS` setting in your `settings.py` file. In our example above, we're using the `auth`, `media`, `debug`, and `i18n` processors. So any variables these libraries set will automatically get added to our context and will be available to our templates.

Using render_to_response with RequestContext

In the last example, we saw how to use the `RequestContext` instead of `Context` in our view function, but how do we do it when we're using `render_to_response`? We don't explicitly define a `Context` object, and so the syntax is slightly different.

In your `mycompany/press/views.py` file, add this import statement to the top of the file:

```
from django.template import RequestContext
```

Alternatively, you can add it to the end of your existing line that imports `Context`. In the same file, edit the `latest` view, changing the highlighted line:

```
def latest(request):
    ''' Returns information on the latest press release '''
    p = PressRelease.objects.latest()
    return render_to_response('press/latest.html', {
        'press': p,
    }, context_instance=RequestContext(request))
```

To use `RequestContext` with `render_to_response`, we simply add an extra argument to the function that tells it what kind of context instance we are using.

Using the context processors in our project

Now that our project is configured to use the default context processors and our view is configured to use `RequestContext`, we can see a context processor in action. Let's see how the `django.core.context_processors.auth` processor can be used with our templates.

In your `mycompany/templates/press/latest.html` file, add the highlighted lines:

```
<html>
<head>
<title>Latest Press Release</title>
</head>
<body>
<hr>
{% if user.is_anonymous %}
  You are not logged in.
{% else %}
  You are logged in as {{ user.username }}.
{% endif %}
<hr>
<h1>{{ press.title }}</h1>
<p>
Author: {{ press.author }}<br/>
Date: {{ press.pub_date }}<br/>
<a href="{{ press.get_absolute_url }}">View Detail</a><br/>
</p>
</body>
</html>
```

Remember that the `auth` processor adds a variable called user to the `RequestContext`, so we can use the `user.is_anonymous` method to see if a user is logged in.

Log in to your site by pointing your browser to the URL `http://localhost:8000/ admin/` and entering your username and password. **Without logging out**, change the URL to `http://localhost:8000/press/latest/`. If you are logged in as the user admin, you should see something similar to this:

Now point your browser to the URL `http://localhost:8000/admin/logout/` and make sure it says you are logged out. Return to the URL `http://localhost:8000/ press/latest/`, and you should see this (you may have to refresh the page):

Writing your own context processor

You're not limited to adding `auth`, `media`, `i18n`, or `debug` to your context. Those are just the default context processors that are included with Django. If you want to include other values in your templates, it is very simple to write your own context processor.

For example, if we wanted to add the user's IP address to the context, we could write our own context processor to do this. Django doesn't care where you put the file that contains your custom context processors as long as it can be imported.

For this example, we'll add a new file in the root of our project. In the `mycompany` directory, add a new file called `context_processors.py` with these lines:

```
def add_ip(request):
    ''' Adds the REMOTE_ADDR value to the context '''
    return {'user_ip_addr': request.META['REMOTE_ADDR']}
```

First, add a reference to our new file in the `TEMPLATE_CONTEXT_PROCESSORS` tuple in your `mycompany/settings.py` file by adding the highlighted line:

```
TEMPLATE_CONTEXT_PROCESSORS = (
    'django.core.context_processors.auth',
    'django.core.context_processors.debug',
    'django.core.context_processors.i18n',
    'django.core.context_processors.media',
    'mycompany.context_processors.add_ip',
)
```

Add the variable `user_ip_addr` at the end of your template (before the `</body>` tag) in the `mycompany/templates/press/lastest.html` file:

```
<hr>User IP: {{ user_ip_addr }}<hr>
```

Point your browser to the URL `http://localhost:8000/press/lastest/`. You should see something similar to this:

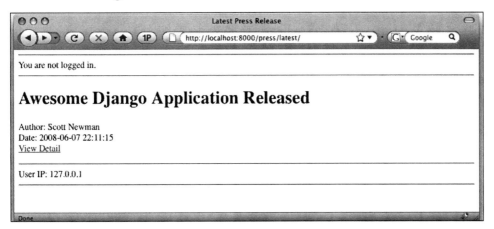

By adding the `add_ip` context processor to our project, we can now access the user's IP address with the `user_ip_addr` variable from any template that is using the `RequestContext`.

Summary

In this chapter, we covered the Django `Context` class and its usage. This was a code-heavy chapter; don't feel bad if you need to go through the chapter again to make sure you got everything.

We saw how to instantiate the `Context` object and pass its values from our views. We briefly looked at manipulating an existing context, and how to use `locals()` to lazily pass all items from our current scope into the Context.

We looked at how to use these values from the context in our templates and how Django handles invalid variables. We also saw some shortcuts for rendering contexts and how to subclass `Context` with the `RequestContext` class to get additional items into our Context.

Next, we'll look at how to use Django's built-in tags and filters.

4
Using the Built-In Tags
and Filters

Django ships with a number of built-in template tags and filters to modify and work with the data in your templates. Recall that filters are used to modify the way data is displayed in templates, such as transforming text to upper or lower case. Tags allow you to execute some logic in your templates, such as looping through data, escaping text for use in JavaScript, and sorting lists.

Most of the common needs of template development are covered using the built-in tags and filters. Unfortunately, not all of them have examples provided in the online documentation, so we'll cover all of them here with examples.

In this chapter, we will explore how to use each of Django's built-in tags and filters with a demonstration of their usage and syntax.

Built-in filter reference

Filters are easier to get your head around than tags, and so we'll start by reviewing them first. If you need to transform the output of your data in the template, you'll use a filter. It's important to remember that they don't modify the data, but only the way it is displayed. If you use the `upper` filter on a template variable, for example, the variable's output will be displayed in the upper case, but the variable's underlying value is not changed. If you use the variable again later in the template without the filter, it will not be displayed in the upper case.

To use a filter, type a pipe symbol after your variable name, then type the filter name, and any arguments it might require. No spaces are put between the variable and the filter name.

For example, if we have a template variable called `myvariable` and we want to use the `upper` filter, it would look like this in the template:

```
{{ myvariable|upper }}
```

add

`add` adds (mathematically, not via concatenation) the argument to the value being modified.

Usage notes:

- `add` requires an integer argument for the value to add, or an argument that can be safely converted to an integer via `int()`.
- It only works with integers. Both the value and the argument are converted to integers when parsed.

Example:

```
{{ myintvalue|add:3 }}
```

Passing a string argument that can be safely converted to an integer also works as follows:

```
{{ myintvalue|add:"3" }}
```

Passing a float argument doesn't throw an exception, but it's converted to an integer, so you'll lose decimal precision. These two examples return the same value:

```
{{ myintvalue|add:3 }}
{{ myintvalue|add:3.5 }}
```

addslashes

This puts a backslash in front of any quotes in the value.

If this value is given:

```
myvalue = 'Django is "the" web app framework'
```

Apply the filter:

```
{{ myvalue|addslashes }}
```

The resulting output will be:

```
Django is \"the\" web app framework
```

capfirst

This capitalizes the first letter of the value being modified.

Usage notes:

- The value being modified must be a string. If you try to modify a numeric value, it won't throw an exception, but will simply ignore it.
- This filter is commonly used for proper nouns when you're not sure the data has been entered that way.

Given this value:

```
myvalue = "this is a good example"
```

Apply the filter:

```
{{ myvalue|capfirst }}
```

Resulting output:

This is a good example

center

This is used to center a value by padding the left and right sides of a string with a whitespace. The total width of the string with whitespace is called the **field**.

Usage note:

- `centre` requires an integer argument (or string that can be cast as an integer) that represents the size of the field.

 Note: If you try this in a browser, remember that browsers ignore multiple spaces and so you won't see the result.

Given this value:

```
myvalue = 'this is a good example'
```

Apply the filter (note the dollar signs at the beginning and end; they are so we can see the effect of the filter):

```
${{ myvalue|center:30 }}$
```

Resulting output:

```
$     this is a good example     $
```

You'll see in the example that the string was 22 characters long, and we told it to center in a field that is 30-characters wide. The filter added 4 spaces to each side of the string, resulting in a centered field 30 characters wide.

cut

This removes the argument from the value being modified (similar to Python's `strip()` function).

Usage notes:

- `cut` requires a string argument representing the string to remove.
- Passing an integer as an argument will throw an exception.

Given this value:

```
myvalue = 'Thank you for not littering and not loitering'
```

Apply the filter:

```
{{ myvalue|cut:"not" }}
```

Resulting output (notice it does not remove the extra spaces).

```
Thank you for  littering and  loitering.
```

date

It formats a `datetime` object to the format specified. The format is the same as the `now` tag we covered earlier.

Usage notes:

- The value being modified must be a `date` or `datetime` object.
- If you are modifying a `date` object (not a `datetime`), you can only pass a format string to use the year, month, and day attributes.
- See the Django online documentation for a full list of all the formatting characters.

Given the value:

```
import datetime
mydate = datetime.datetime.now()
```

Apply the filter:

```
The current year is {{ mydate|date:"Y" }}
```

Resulting output:

```
The current year is 2008
```

default

If the template variable is `False`, this value will be used instead.

Usage notes:

- Works if the value being modified is `False`, `None`, or an empty string.
- If you just want to test for `None`, use the `default_if_none` filter instead.

Given these values:

```
myvalue1 = False
myvalue2 = None
myvalue3 = ''
```

Apply the filter:

```
{{ myvalue1|default:"Value 1 was false" }}<br/>
{{ myvalue2|default:"Value 2 was false" }}<br/>
{{ myvalue3|default:"Value 3 was false" }}<br/>
```

Resulting output:

```
Value 1 was false
Value 2 was false
Value 3 was false
```

default_if_none

Similar to the default tag, this tag will output a default value **only** if the value being modified is `None`.

Given these values:

```
myvalue1 = False
myvalue2 = None
myvalue3 = ''
```

Apply the filter:

```
{{ myvalue1|default_if_none:"Value 1 was false" }}<br/>
{{ myvalue2|default_if_none:"Value 2 was false" }}<br/>
{{ myvalue3|default_if_none:"Value 3 was false" }}<br/>
```

Resulting output: (Notice only the second line returned the default value, while the others returned their actual value.)

```
False
Value 2 was false
```

dictsort

This sorts a list of dictionaries by a specified key.

Usage notes:

- Requires a string argument representing the key to sort by.
- If you try to sort by a key that doesn't exist, it will throw an exception.

Given this value:

```
cars = [
  {'make': 'Ford', 'model': 'Ranger'},
  {'make': 'Chevy', 'model': 'Tahoe'},
  {'make': 'Toyota', 'model': 'Tacoma'},
]
```

Apply the filter:

```
{{ cars|dictsort:"make" }}
```

Resulting output (reformatted to fit the page):

```
[
  {'make': 'Chevy', 'model': 'Tahoe'},
  {'make': 'Ford', 'model': 'Ranger'},
  {'make': 'Toyota', 'model': 'Tacoma'}
]
```

dictsortreversed

This works exactly like the `dictsort` filter, but it sorts in the reverse order.

divisibleby

This returns a Boolean value if the value being modified is divisible by the argument. (This is great for checking if something is even or odd.)

Usage note:

- `divisibleby` requires an integer argument or string that can be safely cast as an integer.

Given this value:

```
myvalue = 100
```

Apply the filter:

```
{{ myvalue|divisibleby:"2" }}
```

Resulting output:

```
True
```

escape

This is used to escape HTML values, transforming <, >, ', ", and & into their HTML character equivalents.

Usage notes:

- If you chain this filter with other filters, `escape` will always happen last. Use the `force_escape` filter if you want it to happen in-place.
- If you apply this filter to a value that is auto-escaped, it will only result in one escaping. (It won't try to do it twice.)

Given this value:

```
myvalue = "Django is <strong>the</strong> best."
```

Apply the filter:

```
{{ myvalue|escape }}
```

Resulting output:

```
Django is &lt;strong&gt;the&lt;/strong&gt; best.
```

escapejs

This is used to escape characters that will be used in dynamically written JavaScript, such as JSON. The characters that can trip up JavaScript are: \\, \, ", >, <, &, =, -, and ;.

Usage notes:

- This filter doesn't escape characters for use in HTML, only JavaScript.
- The filter turns the characters into their hexadecimal equivalents.

Given this value:

```
myvalue = "Django's features are many; it <rules>!"
```

Apply the filter:

```
{{ myvalue1|default:"Value 1 was false" }}<br/>
```

Resulting output:

```
Django\x27s features are many\x3B it \x3Crules\x3E!
```

filesizeformat

This formats a file size to be human-readable (such as KB, MB, etc.).

Usage notes:

- The value being modified must be a `float` or able to be safely cast as a float.
- If the value is less than 1024, it will be returned in bytes.
- If the value is between 1024 and 1048576 (1024 * 1024), it will be returned in kilobytes (KB).
- If the value is between 1048576 and 1073741824 (1024 * 1024 * 1024), it will be returned in megabytes (MB).
- If the value is greater than 1073741824, it will be returned in gigabytes (GB).

Given this value:

```
myvalue = 150000
```

Apply the filter:

```
{{ myvalue|filesizeformat }}
```

Resulting output:

```
146.5 KB
```

first

This returns the first element from a list.

Usage note:

- It requires the value being modified to be a list.

Given this value:

```
mylist = ['Homer', 'Marge', 'Bart', 'Lisa']
```

Apply the filter:

```
{{ mylist|first }}
```

Resulting output:

```
Homer
```

fix_ampersands

This replaces ampersands with their character entity (&)

Usage notes:

- You probably won't use this filter a lot anymore, since the value is auto-escaped in templates by default.
- This is commonly used for instances that require strict adherence to web standards, such as XHTML and XML.

Given this value:

```
Myvalue = "If you're happy & you know it"
```

Apply the filter:

```
{{ myvalue|fix_ampersands }}
```

Resulting output:

```
If you're happy &amp; you know it
```

floatformat

This rounds a `float` value to a given number of decimal places. This filter can be tricky because there are a couple different options available.

Usage notes:

- `floatformat` requires that the value being modified is a float or can safely be cast as a float.
- If you pass no argument to the filter, it will round to one decimal place, but only if there is a decimal value available (that is, 3.00 will round to 3, not 3.0).
- If you pass an integer argument to the filter, it will round to that many places.
- If you pass a negative integer argument to the filter, it will round to that many places, but only if there is a decimal value available.

Given these values:

```
myvalue1 = 3.1234
myvalue2 = 3.00
```

Apply the filters:

```
{{ myvalue1|floatformat:"2" }}
{{ myvalue2|floatformat:"-2" }}
```

Resulting output:

```
3.12
3
```

force_escape

Like the `escape` filter, this filter escapes the HTML values. Unlike the HTML tag, it does it when encountered. (`escape` does it after all other filters.)

If we applied chained filters, we'd get different behavior:

```
{{ myvalue|force_escape|striptags }}
{{ myvalue|escape|striptags }}
```

In the first part of the example, `force_escape` would happen before the `striptags` filter. In the second part, `escape` would happen after the `striptags` filter.

get_digit

This returns the appropriate digit from an integer. The argument represents the number of places to return from the right of the number.

Usage notes:

- If you pass anything other than an integer as an argument to the filter, it won't throw an exception, and returns the original value.

- If you request a position that does not exist (such as "4" in the example below) it will return a zero.

Given the value:

```
myvalue = 987
```

Apply the filter:

```
{{ myvalue|get_digit:"1" }}
```

```
{{ myvalue|get_digit:"3" }}
```

Resulting output:

```
9
7
```

 Note: Think of 2 as the "tens" place, 3 as the "hundreds" place, and so on.

iriencode

This is used to convert **International Resource Identifiers (IRIs)** to safe URL strings. Consult RFC 3987 for more information and examples.

join

This joins a list into a string, similar to Python's `join()` string function.

Usage notes:

- It must be applied to a value that supports iteration.

- It requires a string argument to represent what is to be put between each list element.

Given this value:

```
mylist = ['Eric','Kyle','Stan','Kenny']
```

Apply the filter:

```
{{ mylist|join:", " }}
```

Resulting output:

```
Eric, Kyle, Stan, Kenny
```

last

This returns the last item in a list (similar to the `first` filter).

Usage note:

- It requires the value being modified to be a list.

Given this value:

```
mylist = ['Homer', 'Marge', 'Bart', 'Lisa']
```

Apply the filter:

```
{{ mylist|last }}
```

Resulting output:

```
Lisa
```

length

This returns the length of the value being modified.

Usage notes:

- If the value is a list, it returns the number of items in the list.
- If the value is a string, it returns the string length.

Given these values:

```
mylist = ['Eric','Kyle','Stan','Kenny']
myvalue = 'Garrison'
```

Apply the filters:

```
{{ mylist|length }}
{{ myvalue|length }}
```

Resulting output:

```
4
8
```

length_is

This returns a Boolean indicating if the value is equal to the argument.

Usage note:

- This value requires an integer argument (or value that can be safely cast as an integer).

Given these values:

```
mylist = ['Eric','Kyle','Stan','Kenny']
myvalue = 'Garrison'
```

Apply the filters:

```
{{ mylist|length_is:"4" }}
{{ myvalue|length_is:"10" }}
```

Resulting output:

```
True
False
```

linebreaks

This replaces line breaks with their HTML equivalents.

Usage notes:

- The line breaks become <br />.
- The line breaks followed by a blank line become </p>.
- The value is surrounded with <p></p> tags.

Given the value:

```
myvalue = "This is\n\na good\n example."
```

Apply the filter:

```
{{ myvalue|linebreaks }}
```

Resulting output:

```
<p>This is</p>
<p>a good<br /> example.</p>
```

linebreaksbr

This replaces the newline characters with HTML `<br />` tags. It is similar to the `linebreaks` filter, but it doesn't insert `<p>` tags.

Given the value:

```
myvalue = "This is\na good\n example."
```

Apply the filter:

```
{{ myvalue|linebreaksbr }}
```

Resulting output:

```
This is<br /><br />a good<br /> example.
```

linenumbers

This puts a line number in front of each line.

Usage notes:

- It uses newline characters, not HTML `<br />` or `<p>` tags.
- It doesn't strip out whitespace, so you could end up with spaces at the front of your lines (see the example below).

Given this value:

```
myvalue = "This is\na good\n example."
```

Apply the filter:

```
{{ myvalue|linenumbers }}
```

Resulting output:

```
1. This is
2. a good
3. example.
```

ljust

This is used to left-justify a value by padding the right side of a string with whitespace. The total width of the string with the whitespace is called the "field".

Usage note:

- It requires an integer argument (or string that can be cast as an integer) that represents the size of the field.

 If you try this in a browser, remember that browsers ignore multiple spaces, and so you won't see the result.

Given this value:

```
myvalue = 'this is a good example'
```

Apply the filter (note the dollar signs at the beginning and end; they are so that we can see the effect of the filter):

```
${{ myvalue|ljust:30 }}$
```

Resulting output:

```
$this is a good example        $
```

You'll see in the example that the string was 22 characters long, and we told it to create a field 30 characters wide. The filter added 8 spaces to the right side of the string, resulting in a field 30 characters wide.

lower

This transforms a string to lower case.

Usage note:

- It requires a string argument.

Given this value:

```
myvalue = 'This is a GOOD exAmPlE'
```

Apply the filter:

```
{{ myvalue|lower }}
```

Resulting output:

```
this is a good example
```

make_list

This turns a string or numeric value into a list

- It requires the value being modified to be a string or numeric value.
- It returns a list of Unicode values.

Given these values:

```
myvalue1 = 'Django'
myvalue2 = 123
```

Apply the filter:

```
{{ myvalue1|make_list }}
{{ myvalue2|make_list }}
```

Resulting output:

```
[u'D', u'j', u'a', u'n', u'g', u'o']
[1, 2, 3]
```

phone2numeric

This turns a phone number with letters into the numeric-only version.

Usage notes:

- The value being modified does not have to be a valid phone number or in any special format. Any letters will be transformed into their numeric equivalents.
- Any non-alphabetic character will be returned as is.

Given this value:

```
myvalue = '1-800-ASK-GARY'
```

Apply the filter:

```
{{ myvalue|phone2numeric }}
```

Resulting output:

```
1-800-275-4279
```

pluralize

When applied to a numeric value, this filter can return a suffix that will make the preceding word plural.

Usage notes:

- It requires a numeric value to be modified.
- It returns an "s" to values greater than 1 by default, but you can override the return value for words that are pluralized with "es".

Given this value:

```
num_tools = 11
```

Apply the filter:

```
We have {{ num_tools }} wrench{{ num_tools|pluralize:"es" }}.
```

Resulting output:

```
We have 11 wrenches.
```

pprint

This formats the output in Python's "pretty-printed" format that makes code more readable.

Given this value:

```
cars = [
    {'make': 'Ford', 'model': 'Ranger'},
    {'make': 'Chevy', 'model': 'Tahoe'},
    {'make': 'Toyota', 'model': 'Tacoma'},
]
```

Apply the filter:

```
{{ cars|pprint }}
```

Resulting output:

```
[{'make': 'Ford', 'model': 'Ranger'},
 {'make': 'Chevy', 'model': 'Tahoe'},
 {'make': 'Toyota', 'model': 'Tacoma'}]
```

If we didn't use the pprint filter, the output would look like this (the output is on a single line):

```
[{'make': 'Ford', 'model': 'Ranger'}, {'make': 'Chevy', 'model':
'Tahoe'}, {'make': 'Toyota', 'model': 'Tacoma'}]
```

random

This returns a random element from a list.

Usage note:

- It requires the value being modified to be a list.

Given this value:

```
mylist = [1,2,3,4,5]
```

Apply the filter:

```
{{ mylist|random }}
```

Resulting output: (It could be any item from the list, this time just happened to be 2!)

```
2
```

removetags

This removes a list of HTML/XHTML markup tags from a string.

Usage notes:

- Any text between removed tags is left untouched.
- Arguments to the filter are case sensitive; `<strong>` and `<STRONG>` are distinct searches.
- This is similar to the `striptags` filter, which will remove all tags from a string. `removetags` gives you the choice of what you want to remove.

Given this value:

```
myvalue = 'Django is <strong>the</strong> web app framework'
```

Apply the filter:

```
{{ myvalue|striptags:"strong" }}
```

Resulting output:

```
Django is the web app framework
```

rjust

This is used to right-justify a value by padding the left side of a string with whitespace. The total width of the string with whitespace is called the "field".

Usage notes:

- It requires an integer argument (or string that can be cast as an integer) that represents the size of the field.

 If you try this in a browser, remember that browsers ignore multiple spaces, so you won't see the result.

Given this value:

```
myvalue = 'this is a good example'
```

Apply the filter: (note the dollar signs at the beginning and end, they are so we can see the effect of the filter)

```
${{ myvalue|rjust:30 }}$
```

Resulting output:

```
$ this is a good example$
```

You'll see in the example that the string was 22 characters long, and we told it to create a field 30 characters wide. The filter added 8 spaces to the right side of the string, resulting in a field 30 characters wide.

safe

This tells the template engine not to apply escaping behavior to the string.

Given this value:

```
myvalue = 'Django is <strong>great</strong>'
```

Apply the filter:

```
{{ myvalue|safe }}
```

Resulting output:

```
Django is <strong>great</strong>
```

If we didn't use the safe filter, the output would look like this:

```
Django is &lt;strong&gt;great&lt;/strong&gt;
```

slice

This returns the specified slice of a list.

Usage notes:

- It requires the value being modified to be a list.
- It follows the same rules as Python list slicing. (See online Python documentation for more information, as this can be tricky.)
- It returns a list.

Given this value:

```
mylist = ['Homer', 'Marge', 'Bart', 'Lisa']
```

Apply the filter:

```
{{ mylist|slice:"1:3" }}
```

Resulting output:

```
['Marge', 'Bart']
```

slugify

This transforms a string into a slug by removing non-alphanumeric or underscore characters, replacing spaces with hyphens, and transforming all letters to lower case.

Given this value:

```
myvalue = 'Django is Awesome!'
```

Apply the filter:

```
{{ myvalue|slugify }}
```

Resulting output:

```
django-is-awesome
```

stringformat

This applies a string formatting to a value.

Usage notes:

- It requires a valid string formatting character as an argument.
- See the Python online documentation on string formatting for more information.

Given this value:

```
myvalue = 100
```

Apply the filter:

```
{{ myvalue|stringformat:"s" }}
```

Resulting output:

```
100
```

Though it may not be immediately obvious, the previous example was the same as doing this in Python:

```
myvalue = 100
print "%s" % myvalue
```

striptags

This strips all HTML/XHTML tags from a string.

Usage notes:

- Any values inside of the tags are preserved.
- This filter is similar to the removetags filter, which removes tags in a list you provide.

Given this value:

```
myvalue = 'Django <strong>is</strong> a great<br/> framework'
```

Apply the filter:

```
{{ myvalue|striptags }}
```

Resulting output:

```
Django is a great framework
```

time

This filter formats a Python `time` object to the format specified. The format is the same as the `date` tag we covered earlier, but you can only use format strings that apply to time values, not date values.

timesince

This returns the time between now and the date value being compared. The filter returns value in years, months, days, and minutes.

Usage notes:

- The smallest unit of time returned is minutes.
- It can be applied to `date` or `datetime` objects.
- If you don't want to compare against the current time (now), you can pass a `datetime` object as an argument to use as the comparison date.
- If the value being modified is greater than the current time (or the argument you pass), the filter will return "0 minutes".

Given these values:

```
from datetime import datetime, timedelta
yesterday = datetime.now() - timedelta(days=1)
week_ago = datetime.now() - timedelta(days=7)
```

Apply the filters:

```
{{ yesterday|timesince }}
{{ week_ago|timesince:yesterday }}
```

Resulting output:

```
1 day
6 days
```

timeuntil

This works exactly like the `timesince` tag, but compares times in the future.

title

This transforms the first letter of each word in a string to upper case, also known as "title case".

Given this value:

```
myvalue = 'This is a GOOD exAmPlE'
```

Apply the filter:

```
{{ myvalue|title }}
```

Resulting output:

This Is A Good Example

truncatewords

This truncates a string at a given number of words. (It won't count HTML tags as words if they are present in your string.)

Usage notes:

- It requires an integer argument or an argument that can be safely cast as an integer.
- The filter truncates at word boundaries, not at character counts, and so you can truncate without worrying about returning a partial word.
- Since words can be of varying lengths, you cannot safely cut down a string to a specified length with this filter.
- Returns an ellipsis (...) if the filter successfully truncates a string. (If the string didn't have enough words to truncate, it does not add an ellipsis.)

Given this value:

```
myvalue = "This is a great example of a filter"
```

Apply the filter:

```
{{ myvalue|truncatewords:"3" }}
```

Resulting output:

This is a ...

truncatewords_html

This works the same as the `truncatewords` filter, but it won't leave HTML tags hanging open if it truncates at a place between two tags.

Usage note:

- This filter incurs more of a performance hit than `truncatewords`, so only use if it you have HTML present in your strings.

Given this value:

```
myvalue = "This is a <strong>great example</strong> of it"
```

Apply the filter (note `safe` is being used so as not to escape the HTML tags):

```
{{ myvalue|safe|truncatewords_html:"4" }}
```

Resulting output:

```
This is a <strong>great ...</strong>
```

If you only used `truncatewords` for this, the resulting output would look like this:

```
This is a <strong>great ...
```

unordered_list

This turns lists and nested lists into an HTML unordered list.

Usage notes:

- It won't add the outer `<ul>` and `</ul>` tags for you, so you have to put those outside your template variable being modified.
- It requires that the value being modified is a list.

Given this value:

```
myvalue = ['Homer',['Bart','Lisa','Maggie'],'Ned']
```

Apply the filter:

```
{{ myvalue|unordered_list }}
```

Resulting output:

```
<li>Homer
<ul>
    <li>Bart</li>
    <li>Lisa</li>
```

```
    <li>Maggie</li>
  </ul>
  </li>
  <li>Ned</li>
```

upper

This transforms a string to upper case.

Given this value:

```
myvalue = 'This is a GOOD exAmPlE'
```

Apply the filter:

```
{{ myvalue|upper }}
```

Resulting output:

```
THIS IS A GOOD EXAMPLE
```

urlencode

This escapes a string so that it can be used in a URL. Any characters other than non-alphanumeric characters (a-z, A-Z, 0-9), underscores, and dashes are replaced with their 2-digit hexadecimal equivalent, prefixed with a percent symbol (%).

Usage notes:

- See RFC 1738 for more information on what is allowed in a URL.
- Consult a hex encoding table for information on the hexadecimal equivalents.

Given the value:

```
Myvalue = 'hey! Can you hear me?'
```

Apply the filter:

```
{{ myvalue|urlize }}
```

Resulting output:

```
hey%21%20Can%20you%20hear%20me%3F
```

urlize

This searches for and transforms plain-text web addresses (such as `www.packtpub.com`) into clickable hyperlinks inside of a string.

Usage notes:

- Only apply this filter to plain text, not strings with HTML.
- If HTML is encountered, it won't turn it into a hyperlink but the original text will be returned.
- It adds a `'nofollow'` attribute to the link automatically.
- Doesn't require a subdomain (such as `www`) in front of the text to be recognized as a URL, but you may not get reliable results for domains outside of `.com`, `.net`, and `.org`.

Given this value:

```
myvalue = 'www.abc.com is a good website'
```

Apply the filter:

```
{{ myvalue|urlize }}
```

Resulting output:

```
<a href="http://www.abc.com" rel="nofollow">www.abc.com</a> is a good
website
```

urlizetrunc

This is the same as the `urlize` filter, but it truncates the visible portion of the hyperlink (between the tags) to the specified length.

Usage notes:

- It requires an integer argument for the number of characters to truncate at.
- It inserts an ellipsis (...) when truncating.
- It does not truncate the web address `href` attribute.

Given this value:

```
www.Supercalifragilisticexpialidocious.com rules!
```

Apply the filter:

```
{{ myvalue|urlizetrunc:"10" }}
```

Resulting output:

```
<a href="http://www.Supercalifragilisticexpialidocious.com"
rel="nofollow">www.Supercal...</a> rules!wordcount
```

wordcount

This counts the number of words in a string.

Given this value:

```
Myvalue = 'This is a good example'
```

Apply the filter:

```
{{ myvalue|wordcount }}
```

Resulting output:

```
5
```

wordwrap

This inserts line breaks at the specified character length.

Usage notes:

- It requires an integer argument for the character length.
- Since browsers ignore newlines, you'll probably want to use this inside of a `<pre></pre>` section to preserve formatting.

Given the value:

```
myvalue = 'Long examples are not pretty but short examples can be'
```

Apply the filter:

```
{{ myvalue|wordwrap:"10" }}
```

Resulting output:

```
Long examples
are not pretty
but short
examples can be
```

Notice that it only inserts line breaks. So if you want to insert HTML breaks, you'll need to chain the filters together:

```
{{ myvalue|wordwrap:"10"|linebreaksbr }}
```

Resulting value:

```
Long examples<br />are not pretty<br />but short<br />examples can be
```

yesno

This maps `True`, `False`, and `None` values to specified words.

Usage notes:

- If you don't supply an argument for `None`, `None` will be mapped to the value that `False` uses. (See the third line in the example.)

Given these values:

```
myvalue1 = True
myvalue2 = False
myvalue3 = None
```

Apply these filters:

```
{{ myvalue1|yesno:"Yay,Nay,Ni" }}
{{ myvalue2|yesno:"Yay,Nay,Ni" }}
{{ myvalue3|yesno:"Yay,Nay,Ni" }}
{{ myvalue3|yesno:"Yay,Nay" }}
```

Resulting output:

```
Yay
Nay
Ni
Nay
```

Built-in tag reference

Tags can be trickier to understand than filters because they can do so much more. Tags allow for programming logic in your template code, such as looping through records with the {% for %} tag and performing conditional logic with the {% ifequal %} tag. If you're unsure whether to use a tag or a filter, think about what you're trying to accomplish. If it's simple display formatting, you'll probably use a filter; if it's something more involved, you'll probably need a tag.

To use a tag, you put a single bracket and percent symbol around the tag name. Many tags require an ending tag, such as the `ifequal/endifequal` tag in this example:

```
{% ifequal object.color 'blue' %}
   The object is blue.
{% else %}
  The object is not blue
{% endifequal %}
```

autoescape

This turns on or off the auto-escaping behavior in a Django template block. When escaping is enabled, HTML characters are turned into their character equivalents to prevent potentially malicious content from being written.

Usage Notes:

- It requires the ending tag `endautoescape`.
- It requires a single string argument `on` or `off`.
- This tag is similar to the `escape` filter covered earlier.

For example, if we set this template variable in our view:

```
test = 'This is my <script>alert("content");</script>!'
```

If the value isn't escaped, the JavaScript will execute and a dialog box will be presented:

```
{% autoescape off %}
  {{ test }}
{% endautoescape %}
```

This was a benign example, but you can imagine the implications of malicious JavaScript code being executed. By default, templates autoescape the values of template variables, and so this tag is useful when you want to dynamically output HTML content.

block

This delimits a section of Django template for use with template inheritance.

Usage Notes:

- It requires a single string argument that is the name of the block.
- It requires the ending tag `endblock`.
- The `endblock` tag can optionally have the name of the block as an argument.

Example:

```
{% block page_content %}
  This is my page content.
{% endblock page_content %}
```

comment

This is used to prevent the Django template engine from evaluating template code. It's similar to HTML comment tags, but the commented code will not be included in the response. This tag is great for debugging sections of template code.

Usage note:

- It requires the ending tag `endcomment`.

Example:

```
{% comment %}
  None of this will be parsed:
  {{ bad_variable }}
{% endcomment %}
```

cycle

This is used to alternate through a list of variables or strings. It's often used in a loop, but you can also use it to alternate through values as they are encountered in the template.

Usage notes:

- Arguments to the tag can be strings or template variables.
- If used outside of a loop, you'll need to use an argument to name the value being cycled.

Example (in a loop):

```
<table>
{% for val in val_list %}
  <tr bgcolor="{% cycle 'white' 'green' %}">
    <td>My row</td>
  </tr>
{% endfor %}
</table>
```

Each iteration through the loop will alternate the values `white` and `green` as the background color for the row.

You don't have to use the `cycle` tag in a loop. You can define a name for the alternating values and call them using the `cycle` tag again:

```
{% cycle 'white' 'green' as mycolors %}
<p>My first color is: {% cycle mycolors %}</p>
<p>My second color is: {% cycle mycolors %}</p>
```

debug

This returns a set of huge dictionaries with debugging information. This is very useful when you're trying to figure out if a value is in the current context.

Example:

```
{% debug %}
```

extends

This tells the template engine that the template is the child of another template. All the blocks in this template will be "carried up" into the parent.

Usage note:

- It requires a string or template variable argument that indicates what template is being extended.

Example:

```
{% extends "section_base.html" %}
{% block content %}
  I am a child template.
{% endblock %}
```

filter

This is used to apply a template filter to a section of content between the tags. Template filters are traditionally applied to template variables, but this allows you to run them on a whole section of content, including multiple variables.

Usage notes:

- It requires an argument telling the tag what filter to apply.
- You can chain filters together using a pipe.

Example:

```
{% filter upper %}
  everything between the tags will be upper-cased.
  {{ myvar1 }} is upper-cased, so is {{ myvar2 }}.
{% endfilter %}
```

You can chain filters together:

```
{% filter upper|truncatewords:2 %}
  you won't see more than two words, but they
  will be upper-cased!
{% endfilter %}
```

firstof

This returns the first variable that isn't **False**.

Usage notes:

- It requires at least one template variable as an argument. (If you pass as a string, there's no way for it to return **False**, so that doesn't make sense to do.)

- If all of your arguments are **False**, the tag doesn't return anything.

- You can pass a string as a last argument and it will be used as a default value if none of the preceding arguments are returned.

- Though it would seem like you could, you cannot pass a list as a single argument and have it evaluate the values of the list; the tag will return the whole list.

If we set these values in our view:

```
val1 = None
val2 = 'Something'
```

We can use the `firstof` tag to return them:

```
{% firstof val1 val2 "default" %}
```

Because `val1` is `None` and will return `False`, the value `Something` will be returned.

for

This loops through an iterable variable, most commonly a list.

Usage notes:

- It requires an iterable argument.
- It requires an `endfor` closing tag.
- You can loop through a variable in reverse order by passing the argument `reversed`.
- You can unpack the iterated variables as you loop through them (see the example that will follow).
- The `forloop` variable gives you access to information about the current loop (current position, if the current item is first/last, number of iterations until the end).

Example:

```
{% for item in item_list %}
  {{ item }}
{% endfor %}
```

If you want to loop through a list backwards, you can pass the `reversed` argument:

```
{% for item in item_list reversed %}
  {{ item }}
{% endfor %}
```

If the values in your iterable can be unpacked, you can do so and use the values. This is useful for looping through a dictionary and getting both the key and the value:

```
{% for key, val in mydict %}
  The current key is {{ key }},
  the value is: {{ val }}
{% endfor %}
```

forloop

A `forloop` variable is automatically created when you are looping through an iterable. You can use its properties to get information about the loop:

- `forloop.first`: This returns `True` if this is the first iteration of the loop.
- `forloop.last`: This returns `True` if this is the last iteration of the loop.
- `forloop.counter`: This shows the current iteration of the loop (that is, where you are in the loop).
- `forloop.revcounter`: This shows the number of iterations until the end of the loop.
- `forloop.parentloop`: This shows information about the parent loop in a nested loop.

Here's an example of how to use the `forloop` variable:

```
{% for item in mylist %}
  {% if forloop.first %}
    # of items: {{ forloop.revcounter }}<br/>
  {% endif %}
  {{ item }}{% if not forloop.last %},{% endif %}
{% endfor %}
```

If the value of `mylist` was equal to `['eggs', 'milk', 'butter', 'salt']`, the resulting output of this example would look like this:

```
# of items: 4<br/>
eggs, milk, butter, salt
```

We use the `last` property to make sure that we don't have a trailing comma in our output.

 The properties `counter` and `revcounter` are "1-indexed", meaning the first value is 1. If you want the first value to be 0, use the properties `counter0` and `revcounter0` instead.

if

This executes a section of template code if the argument is `True`.

Usage notes:

- "`true`" passes for multiple conditions: Boolean `True`, a `non-None` variable, and a non-empty list.
- There is no `'else-if'` functionality, but you can nest your `if` tags.
- You can use `and` and `or` to perform multiple evaluations.
- You can use `not` to check negative equality.
- It requires an `endif` closing tag.

The "`true`"-ness of a value can be confusing, so let's break it down. We'll say an item "passes" when the `if` tag evaluates it as true:

Boolean values:

```
myvalue1 = True # Passes
myvalue2 = False # Does not pass
```

String values:

```
myvalue1 = 'Good book' # Passes
myvalue2 = '' # Does not pass
```

Non-None values:

```
myvalue1 = None # Does not pass
```

List values:

```
myvalue1 = [1,2,3] # Passes
myvalue2 = [] # Does not pass
```

Use and to test that multiple values are all true:

```
{% if myvalue1 and myvalue2 %}
  passes if both variables are true
{% endif %}
```

Use or to test that multiple values have at least one item that is true:

```
{% if myvalue1 or myvalue2 %}
  passes if one of the variables is true
{% endif %}
```

Use not to check if the value does not evaluate to true:

```
{% if not myvalue1 %}
  There was no value.
{% endif %}
```

ifchanged

This tests to see if a variable's value has changed since the last iteration through a loop. This tag is commonly used when iterating through a list of objects and you want start a new section of output when a value changes.

Usage notes:

- It requires a template value argument representing the value to compare between loops.
- You can check to see if multiple values have changed by passing multiple arguments.
- You can use an else tag to perform an action if the value hasn't changed.
- It also requires a closing endifchanged tag.

For example, if you have a class schedule and you want to split it up by rooms, you could do something like this:

```
{% for course in course_list %}
  {% ifchanged course.location %}
    <h1>{{ course.location }}</h1>
  {% endifchanged %}
{% endfor %}
```

On the first iteration through the list, `course.location` will register as changed because there was no preceding value to check. So, you don't have to worry about checking if it's the first time through the list.

If you want to perform an action when multiple items have changed, you can pass more than one argument to the tag:

```
{% for course in course_list %}
  {% ifchanged course.campus course.name %}
    <h1>{{ course.name }}</h1>
  {% else %}
    {{ course.name }}
  {% endifchanged %}
```

In this example, the course name will be in header tags if both the campus and name are different than the previous iteration.

For this technique to be effective, you'll want to make sure the lists are ordered by the property being compared. If you don't, you'll have multiple headers for the same value.

See the `regroup` tag for similar functionality. We'll cover that tag shortly.

ifequal

This checks to see if the two arguments are equal. One important catch with this tag is that you can't check if a value is equal to `True` or `False`. You can only test the equality of values. If you need to check `True` or `False`, use the `if` tag instead.

Usage notes:

- It requires two arguments to compare, one of which may be a string. (It wouldn't make sense to compare two strings.)
- Both arguments can be template variables.

- You can use `else` to perform an action if the two values are not equal.
- It requires a closing `endifequal` tag.

   You can test if a value is equal to None.

Example:

```
{% ifequal course.name 'Algebra' %}
  This is algebra.
{% else %}
  This is not algebra.
{% endifequal %}
```

ifnotequal

This is exactly like the `ifequal` tag, but checks if the arguments do not equal each other.

include

This is used to load a template into the current template and render it with the current context.

Usage notes:

- It requires a single string or template variable argument that tells the tag what template file to load.
- The path to the template file is not relative to the current template.
- Any template variables in the included file are rendered with the current context.

Example:

```
{% include 'sports/stats.html' %}
```

In the preceding example, the file `sports/stats.html` is relative to the `TEMPLATE_ DIRS` setting. So if the `include` tag was used in the `sports/news.html` file, you still have to tell it to look in the `sports` directory.

You can also use a template variable as the argument to the `include` tag so that you can dynamically include files.

load

This loads a custom tag or filter library.

Usage notes:

- Django looks for directories called `templatetags`, when it initializes and searches through them, when the `load` tag calls a library.
- You don't have to specify the directory a library exists in.
- You don't put quotes around the library name.
- You can pass multiple tag libraries as arguments.

Example:

```
{% load blogs_extratags %}
```

You can pass multiple arguments to the load tag, putting a space between each:

```
{% load blogs_extratags news_extratags %}
```

now

This displays the current date/time stamp. You can customize it using defined format strings.

Usage notes:

- It requires a string argument to define the format of the output.
- There are a few dozen format strings available, and we'll briefly look at a few of them. (See the online documentation for a full reference.)
- To add literal values into the format string, prefix it with a backslash.

Here are a few string values and what they return:

- Y: Four-digit year
- l: Day name (in a long format such as Monday, Friday, etc.)
- f: Time in hours and minutes (such as 4:15)
- F: Month name (in a long format such as January, November, etc.)
- j: Day of the month without leading zeros
- S: Day of the month suffix (such as "rd", "th", and so on)

For example, Y will return the current year with four digits:

```
The current year is {% now "Y" %}.
```

You can use multiple strings inside the formatting argument. Notice the comma that is added to the output as a string literal:

```
Today is {% now "l, F jS" %}
```

This example displays something like this:

Today is Sunday, August 31st

If you want to include a literal string value that clashes with one of the built-in formatting characters, put a slash in front of it:

```
Today is the {% "now jS o\f F" %}
```

This example displays the following:

Today is the 31st of August

If we didn't put a slash in front of f, the template would think we wanted the value that f returns, which is the time in hours and minutes:

Today is the 31st 08:16 August

There are dozens of formatting characters available. Consult the online Django documentation for a full list.

regroup

This takes a list of objects and groups them by a common attribute. This is one of the trickier tags to work with.

Usage notes:

- It requires three arguments: the name of the list to group, the attribute to group by, and the list that will be returned by the tag.
- The returned value is a list of dictionaries with the keys list and grouper. list is the resulting list and grouper is the attribute that list was grouped by.

Let's use a list of academic courses as an example. In our view, we set these values:

```
course_list = [
    {'name': 'Art', 'instructor': 'Skinner'},
    {'name': 'Physics', 'instructor': 'Skinner'},
    {'name': 'Math', 'instructor': 'Hoover'},
    {'name': 'Astronomy', 'instructor': 'Crabapple'},
    {'name': 'Gym', 'instructor': 'Chalmers'},
    {'name': 'Physics', 'instructor': 'Hoover'},
]
```

Let's return the list of courses grouped by the instructor's name. First, we'll call the `regroup` tag with the proper arguments:

```
{% regroup course_list by instructor as regrouped_courses %}
```

In this example, `course_list` is the original list we're working with, `instructor` is the attribute from the list we want to group by, and `regrouped_courses` is the value that will be returned by the `regroup` tag.

Next, we'll use a `for` loop to iterate over the regrouped course list that was returned in the previous example:

```
{% for item in regrouped_courses %}
<h1>{{ item.grouper }}</h1>
{% for course in item.list %}
  {{ course.name }}<br/>
{% endfor %}
{% endfor %}
```

Here's the part that can seem tricky. Each element of `regrouped_courses` is a dictionary with two keys:

- grouper
- list

In this example, `item.grouper` returns the instructor name (that's the item we regrouped by in the previous example). `item.list` is the list of grouped objects related to the `grouper`.

As with the `ifchanged` tag, you must start with sorted data to get reliable results. The most efficient way is to specify the proper ordering when retrieving results with the database API, but there is a `dictsort` filter that can be used to sort dictionaries from within the template. We covered that filter earlier in the chapter.

spaceless

This removes the whitespace that surrounds and is between HTML tags, including tab and newline characters.

Usage notes:

- It requires a closing `endspaceless` tag.
- It doesn't remove whitespace from inside tags, but only between tags.

Example:

```
{% spaceless %}
   <strong>
      <p>Django Rules</p>
   </strong>
{% endspaceless %}
```

This example returns the following output:

```
<strong><p>Django Rules</p></strong>
```

ssi

Similar to the `include` tag, this tag brings in the contents of the given page into the current template.

Usage notes:

- It requires an argument with absolute path to the file that you wish to include.
- You can specify an optional argument `parsed` to parse the included file with the current context.
- You must have the path to be included specified in the `ALLOWED_INCLUDE_ROOTS` tuple in your `settings.py` file.

Though this tag looks very similar to the `include` tag, there are two key differences:

- The `ssi` tag does not parse the contents of the file unless you specify the optional argument `parsed` (see the example ahead).
- The file to be included is independent of your `TEMPLATE_DIRS` setting. The tag takes an absolute file system path.

Example:

```
{% ssi '/projects/mycompany/templates/menu.html' parsed %}
```

templatetag

This allows you to write out the characters used to work with template tags.

Usage note:

- It requires a string argument specifying the characters you wish to output.

The immediate usage of this is not obvious until you try to write something like this in your template:

```
In order to load your tag library, use this command:
{% load mytag %}
```

If you tried to write this, you'd get a template syntax error that the tag `'mytag'` couldn't be opened, or if it were a valid tag, it would simply load the library and return nothing.

If you want to write out a literal output such as the example above, use the `templatetag` tag with the appropriate arguments:

```
In order to load your tag library, use this command:
{% templatetag openblock %}
load mytag
{% templatetag closeblock %}
```

The available arguments and characters they output are:

- openblock: {%
- closeblock: %}
- openbrace: {
- closebrace: }
- opencomment: {#
- closecomment: #}
- openvariable: {{
- closevariable: }}

Now when the template is rendered, `{% template openblock %}` will be replaced with {% and `{% template closeblock %}` will be replaced with %}.

url

This is used with a reverse URL matching to return a URL path without having to hardcode a URL into your template.

Usage notes:

- It requires an argument specifying a URL pattern to match.
- An optional second argument takes a comma-separated list and inserts the items as needed into the URL (see the example overleaf).
- You must specify all the arguments a URL configuration is expecting, such as ID and slug values.

For example, if the list of press releases on your site is located at /press/list/, you don't want to hardcode that URL into your templates in case it changes in the future. Instead, you can use the url tag to "look up" the appropriate URL pattern and output it into your template.

Suppose you have a URL configuration like this:

```
url(r'detail/(?P<pid>\d+)/$', 'press.views.detail',
   name='press_detail')
```

You can use the url tag to find the URL configuration associated with the press detail view:

```
{% url press.views.detail 4 %}
```

This example will return this output:

```
/press/releases/4
```

If you are using named patterns in your URL configuration, you can specify the name of the configuration instead of the view as the argument to the tag. You will get the same result as above with this example:

```
{% url press_detail 4 %}
```

It's a good idea to use named URL patterns if you are going to use the url tag in case you have multiple URL configurations that point to the same view.

widthratio

This computes the ratio of a given value to a maximum value. This tag was made for creating bar charts (hence the "width" part of the name), but it can be used to calculate percentages.

Usage notes:

- For creating bar charts, the tag requires three arguments: a given value, the total max value, and the length of the bar in the chart.
- For creating percentages, the tag also requires three arguments: a given value, the max value, and 100 (you multiply by 100 to get the percentage of 100).

For example, when creating a chart, if the given value val is 50, the highest value maxval is 100, and the length of the bar is 200 pixels, you'd write the tag like this:

```
<img src="chart.gif" width="{% widthratio val maxval 200 %}">
```

The example would output the following because 50/100 * 200 = 100 pixels:

```
<img src="chart.gif" width="100">
```

To calculate a percentage, the syntax is similar. Let's say we're figuring out the percentage of people that voted "YES" on a poll. If 50 people voted "YES" (represented by `yes_votes`), and 200 people voted (represented by `total_votes`), then we'd calculate it like this:

```
Yes votes: {% widthratio yes_votes total_votes 100 %}
```

In this example, the output would be 25%. (50 "YES" votes / 200 total votes * 100)

with

This takes a computed variable and stores it as a template variable. If you have a value that needs to be computed and used multiple times in a template, you can compute it once and store it, reusing it as necessary without having to calculate it again. This is beneficial if the computation of the value is processor or memory intensive.

Usage notes:

- It requires two arguments: the computed value and the name under which to store it.
- The stored variable is only available within the `with` and `endwith` tags.
- It requires the closing `endwith` tag.

This tag is also useful if you need to run a template filter on a variable, as you only have to do it once.

Example:

```
{% with myname|upper as myuppername %}
  <p>Hello, I'm {{ myuppername }}.</p>
  <p>{{ myuppername }} welcomes you.}}</p>
{% endwith %}
```

This example is trivial, but if you have a template variable that requires a database-intensive lookup or expensive filter (such as an intensive regular expression on a long text field) it can help your performance.

Summary

This was a very long chapter, but should serve as an important reference as you begin using the built-in tags and filters in your templates. We reviewed all the tags and filters that come with Django and explored an example of the usage and syntax for each.

In the next chapter, we'll look at how to load and inherit templates in your application.

5
Loading and Inheriting Templates

In order to use our templates, Django needs to know how we want to load them from the filesystem and where the template files can be found. In the first chapter we briefly looked at how this worked in order to get some examples working. So now let's take a closer look at how the system works.

In this chapter we will:

- Explore the configuration options to set up the template system
- Learn the different methods for loading templates
- Create templates for error handling
- Extend templates using inheritance
- Create parent and child templates
- Create a strategy for setting up templates in your projects
- Work with template includes

Configuring the template system

There are a number of configuration settings for your `mycomapny/settings.py` file, but there are only four main ones we need to work out with to configure the Django template system: `DEBUG`, `TEMPLATE_DEBUG`, `TEMPLATE_LOADERS`, and `TEMPLATE_DIRS`.

DEBUG

The `DEBUG` setting tells Django to run in debugging mode, enabling diagnostic information to be displayed in the browser when errors occur. These error messages can be very helpful for tracking down errors and bugs.

Here's how it should look in your `mycompany/settings.py` file:

```
DEBUG = True
    TEMPLATE_DEBUG = True
```

When debugging is turned off, errors will be displayed using a friendly error template instead of showing the diagnostic information that you wouldn't want general users to see. By default, Django hides the most sensitive settings. But there are still bits of information you probably don't want the users to see.

Here's an example of debugging output:

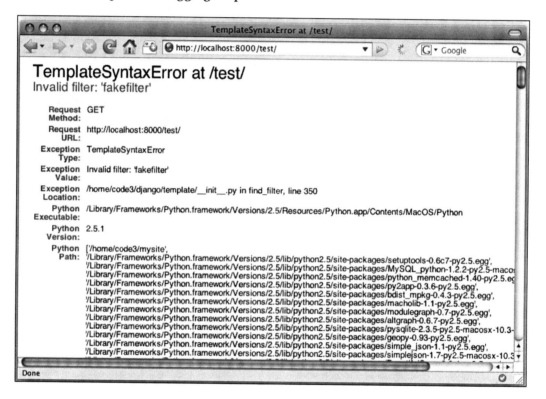

 Caution: DEBUG also controls extra SQL logging and it can be a real memory hog when enabled. Debugging should be disabled in production applications for both performance and security.

TEMPLATE_DEBUG

The `TEMPLATE_DEBUG` setting enables the template debugging mode where extra detail will be displayed for template syntax errors.

Here's how it should look in your `mycompany/settings.py` file:

```
DEBUG = True
TEMPLATE_DEBUG = DEBUG
```

Since the template debugging information is only shown when `DEBUG` is `True`, both settings have to be `True` to take advantage of this setting.

The **Template error** section in the following example is only shown when `TEMPLATE_DEBUG` is equal to `DEBUG`:

TEMPLATE_LOADERS

The `TEMPLATE_LOADERS` setting is a tuple that tells Django how you are going to load templates, either from specified directories on the filesystem, from subdirectories under each of your applications, or from Python Eggs. We will look at the differences later in the chapter.

A *tuple* is a Python native datatype similar to a list. But once defined, the tuple cannot have items added to it, removed from it, or have its values changed. They generally offer better performance than lists. You can find more information about tuples and Python datatypes at www.python.org/docs or www.diveintopython.com.

Here's how it should look in your mycompany/settings.py file:

```
TEMPLATE_LOADERS = (
    'django.template.loaders.filesystem.load_template_source',
    'django.template.loaders.app_directories.load_template_source',
#    'django.template.loaders.eggs.load_template_source',
)
```

TEMPLATE_DIRS

The TEMPLATE_DIRS setting is a tuple that specifies where on the filesystem the template files are found. You should always end the path with a trailing slash.

Here's how it should look in your mycompany/settings.py file:

```
TEMPLATE_DIRS = (
    '/projects/mycompany/templates/',
)
```

If you are using a Windows machine, you need to use Unix-style forward slashes in your paths:

```
TEMPLATE_DIRS = (
 'c:/projects/mycompany/templates/',
)
```

As we discussed in Chapter 1, this is one of the few settings that need to be changed if you're using a Windows machine to develop your code.

Finding a home for the template files

Template files can be located anywhere on the filesystem, provided the web server has the appropriate permission to read the directory and files within. It's a common practice in Django development to make a directory for your templates with subdirectories for each of your application's templates.

In our ongoing example project, we created a directory at mycompany/templates and created a press subdirectory underneath it.

For some projects with many developers, it might make more sense to keep your template files in a completely separate location away from your code, such as /projects/html. This way, you can easily set special permissions on these files or give template authors a separate place on the filesystem to work, which keeps them completely out of your code.

Working with the template loaders

Django's template loaders ease the burden of working with template files on the filesystem. You just tell the loader which template file to use and the rest is taken care of. Before we look at the actual loaders, let's look at why we want to use them.

Loading templates manually

If you didn't use a loader, you'd have to write a slew of Python code when working with template files. In order to load a file manually, you'd have to:

- Check for the existence of the template file
- Check that you have permissions to open the template file
- Code exception handling if the file doesn't exist or you can't read it
- Write open(), read(), and close() methods on the file handle every time you want to use it
- Pass the file contents into the template loader

Not only is this tedious, it's boring, messy, and error-prone. Consider these two code samples:

Without template loader:

```
try:
    f = open(os.path.join(settings.TEMPLATE_DIRS[0]),
        'press/demo.html')
    data = f.read()
    f.close()
except IOError, e:
    return HttpResponseServerError('Error Loading Template')

t = Template(data)
return HttpResponse(t.render(c))
```

With the template loader:

```
t = loader.get_template('press/demo.html')
return HttpResponse(t.render(c))
```

The template loader provides a clean, consistent, and common way to load templates that also handles the various errors that could happen.

Choosing a template loader

There are three different types of loaders available to our projects, allowing us to get our template files in different ways:

- Load from specified directories on the filesystem
- Load from the application directories
- Load from Python Eggs

When you first create your project, all three loader types are made available in the `settings.py` file:

```
TEMPLATE_LOADERS = (
    'django.template.loaders.filesystem.load_template_source',
    'django.template.loaders.app_directories.load_template_source',
#    'django.template.loaders.eggs.load_template_source',
)
```

We saw this code snippet at the beginning of the chapter when talking about the `TEMPLATE_DIRS` setting.

 The eggs loader is commented out by default. In practice, it's rarely used and you can safely remove it from the tuple if you aren't planning to use it.

Using the filesystem loader

The `filesystem` loader is the most common way to load templates. It uses the paths specified in the `TEMPLATE_DIRS` setting to find your template files. Let's look at an example using our ongoing project.

In the `mycompany/settings.py` file, make sure your `TEMPLATE_DIRS` tuple is pointing to the `templates` directory:

```
TEMPLATE_DIRS = (
    '/projects/mycompany/templates/',
)
```

In the `mycompany/press/views.py` file, look at the `loader.get_template` call:

```
def detail(request, pid):
    '''
    Accepts a press release ID and returns the detail page
    '''
    p = get_object_or_404(PressRelease, id=pid)
    t = loader.get_template('press/detail.html')
    c = Context({'press': p})
    return HttpResponse(t.render(c))
```

Django will use the path from the `TEMPLATE_DIRS` setting joined with the argument to `get_template` to figure out that the template is located here on the filesystem:

```
/projects/mycompany/templates/press/detail.html
```

The `TEMPLATE_DIRS` setting can have specific multiple filesystem paths for templates. (In most applications, you probably will only have one or two paths.) The loader will try each of the paths listed when looking for a template, using the first one it finds.

Using the application directories loader

You can use the `app_directories` loader to load templates from subdirectories underneath your individual application directories. The template system looks for directories called `templates` under each of your applications listed in the configuration setting `INSTALLED_APPS` in your `mycompany/settings.py` file.

For example, in our application at `mycompany/press`, the `app_directories` loader would look for a folder called `mycompany/press/templates`. When we tried to load the template in our view above, Django would try to find our template in this directory:

```
/projects/mycompany/press/templates/detail.html
```

To maximize the performance, Django looks through all the applications during initialization and caches a list of which apps have subdirectories called `templates`. The only performance penalty will be on the initial startup. After that, Django will use the cached list of directories when looking for templates.

> The `app_directories` loader doesn't even look at the `TEMPLATE_DIRS` setting.

Using the `app_directories` loader is useful when you are planning to write an application that is shared with others or becomes part of a library. In those cases, the templates are distributed along with the application and it "just works" out of the box.

The disadvantage to this approach is that your template files are spread throughout your project in individual application directories and this makes maintenance more difficult. If you're not planning to distribute or reuse your application in multiple sites, you probably will find it's better to use the `filesystem` loader.

 Caution: In case you are thinking "I'll never use the `app_directories` loader, I think I'll just take it out...", be aware that Django's admin application needs it to load its default templates.

About the eggs template loader

The `eggs` loader is commented out by default and is not in widespread use. It's made for application authors who share their applications as Python Eggs. Similar to the `app_directories` loader, you can put your template files inside your distributable application and the loader will look inside the egg (usually nested deep under the Python folder on your system) for the template.

With its extremely specific appeal, we're not going to spend time covering this topic. Just know that it is one of the available template choices and it's there if you need it.

Using the loaders together

Because you can specify more than one loader type, Django will try them in the order you specified in the TEMPLATE_LOADERS setting. It's common practice to use both the `filesystem` and `app_directories` loader types in projects.

This is how it is set up by default. We left it as is for our `mycompany/settings.py` file:

```
TEMPLATE_LOADERS = (
    'django.template.loaders.filesystem.load_template_source',
    'django.template.loaders.app_directories.load_template_source',
#    'django.template.loaders.eggs.load_template_source',
)
```

Using this setup, `filesystem` is the first loader type, and `app_directories` is the second. If Django can't find the template in one of the paths in TEMPLATE_DIRS, it will try looking in the folders underneath each application in your project.

Loading your template files

Regardless of the loader type used, you will use one of two methods inside your views to retrieve your templates: `get_template` or `select_template`.

The `get_template` method is what we have been using so far. It takes a single argument, the name of the template to load, and it handles all the dirty work of file locating, opening, reading, closing, and exception handling. You can also pass it the subdirectory names in the argument:

```
t = loader.get_template('detail.html')
t = loader.get_template('press/detail.html')
```

The `select_template` method works just like `get_template`, but instead of taking a single path to a template file, you pass it a list of file paths:

```
t = loader.select_template(['demo/override.html',
    'demo/press.html'])
```

The template loader will try each file path in the list until a match is found. If the file is not found or is not valid, no exceptions are thrown. The template engine moves on and tries the next file listed. This is a very important concept because it allows us to override default templates on demand.

Hypothetically, if your model has a field called `template_override`, it allows you to (optionally) specify a custom template on a per-record basis. When you retrieve the data from your model, you can pass the value of that field as the first item in the list to `select_template` like this:

```
m = Myobject.objects.get(id=1)
t = loader.select_template([m.template_override,
    'press/detail.html'])
```

In this code snippet, if `m.template_override` has no value (or specifies an invalid template file), the loader will load the `press/detail.html` file.

Setting up the error handling templates

When Django encounters an error and needs to serve a 404 (Page Not Found) or 500 (Server Error) response, it looks for the files called `404.html` and `500.html` (respectively) in the root of your templates directory. If you have more than one directory in your `TEMPLATE_DIRS` setting, it will search each one in order until it finds the required file.

If it can't find the `404.html` file, Django will serve a `TemplateDoesNotExist` error. If it can't find the `500.html` file, you'll get the most generic-looking error page your web server provides.

 If you have debugging enabled in your `settings.py` file, Django will serve you a diagnostic error page and you won't see your `404.html` or `500.html` templates.

Creating the error templates

Let's add these error pages to our project. Create a new file called `404.html` in the `mycompany/templates` directory and add these lines:

```
<html>
<head>
<title>Page Not Found</title>
</head>
<body>
<h1>Page Not Found</h1>
</body>
</html>
```

Create a new file called `500.html` in the `mycompany/templates` directory and add these lines:

```
<html>
<head>
<title>Error</title>
</head>
<body>
<h1>An Error Has Occurred</h1>
</body>
</html>
```

Testing the error templates

To test our templates, we'll have to temporarily turn off debugging for our project. To do this, edit your `mycompany/settings.py` file and set `DEBUG` to `False`:

```
DEBUG = False
```

Point your browser to the URL `http://localhost:8000/badurl/` (or something else that doesn't exist in our project), and you should see the output of your `404.html` template.

You can intentionally introduce an error into one of your project files (such as an unindented line or misplaced character) if you want to test your 500.html template.

Make sure you set DEBUG back to True in your settings.py file when you are done testing these templates.

Breaking templates into reusable pieces

Up to this point, we have been working with template files that were self-contained. This was good for explaining the theory behind working with templates, but in reality your templates will share common parts with each other such as headers, footers, and menus.

Typically, in web application development (regardless of the language or platform) this is solved by dynamically inserting other files into your template (known as "include" files in many systems). When a template is loaded, it "calls in" content from various files and inserts it in the appropriate places. This approach does not lend itself well to complex setups where your included file needs to inject content into multiple places in your base template. (It can be done, but it's typically not very simple.)

Django gives us a very flexible way to break up our templates, which solves the challenges of complex include files, called *template inheritance*. Instead of filling holes in your base template with the content from included files, you take your current template and put its contents into the holes in a parent template (the reverse of an *include* file).

Extending templates with inheritance

With template extension, you create labeled "blocks" in your parent templates that get filled with content from child templates. Let's illustrate this with a diagram:

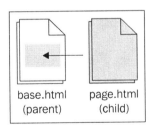

base.html   page.html
(parent)   (child)

Notice that the arrow is pointing from the child template to the parent template. In Django templates, you start from a child template and work up into parent templates. In this example, the view would load and parse `page.html`, and the rendered output from `page.html` would go into `base.html` via logic in the template file.

Looking at the diagram, `base.html` (the parent template) has a "hole" where the output of `page.html` (the child template) goes. The hole in the parent is labeled with a `block` tag so that it can be identified by the child. The label tells the template engine, "This area can be replaced by content in a child template *if* you have it."

Using the block tag

In the diagram we say that `page.html` *extends* `base.html`. To accomplish this, we're going to make a hole in `base.html` that will get filled with the contents of `page.html`. We'll use a template tag called `block` to define where that hole is and what it is called.

The `block` tag takes a single argument, the name of the block. The template engine uses this name to match up a block in a child template with a block in the parent template. Block tags require a matching tag `endblock` to define the end of the content.

The important thing to remember is that there are two block tags, one in the child and one in the parent. Anything in the child's block tag gets put into the parent's block tag. We'll look at some basic examples here and then add these concepts to our press application to bring it all together.

Here's an example of what the `block` tag looks like:

```
{% block content %}
  This is my page content.
{% endblock content %}
```

 You don't have to use the name of the block in the `endblock` tag, but it's a good idea to label it to keep things identifiable.

The `base.html` file is the parent template and looks like this:

```
<html>
<head>
<title>Press Release</title>
</head>
<body>
{% block content %}{% endblock content %}
</body>
</html>
```

Notice the area under the `<body>` tag where we put the block tag called `content`. We're telling the template engine that child templates can override the contents of this area. When the engine finds a block called `content` in a child template, it will stick the contents of that block in this area.

The `page.html` file is the child template and looks like this:

```
{% extends "base.html" %}

{% block content %}
  This is the body of my press release.
{% endblock content %}
```

Notice that this template also has a `block` tag in it labeled `content`. In fact, that's really all this template has except for the `extends` tag (which we'll get to soon).

I've added in some `html` comments for clarity. When we look at the rendered output, we'll use them to see where the contents of the block start and end.

When the page is rendered, the source looks like this:

```
<html>
<head>
<title>Press Release</title>
</head>
<body>
This is the body of my press release.
</body>
</html>
```

How did this work? Let's break it down. In our parent template (`base.html`) we left a hole in the middle that we expected to be filled by a child template (`page.html`).

That hole was defined as a block called `content` that held the body of our press release. The contents of the block labeled `content` were carried up to the template and put in the matching hole labeled `content`.

Extending templates

When the template engine renders the child template, the first tag found in the template is the `extends` tag. This tells the template engine that this template is a child of another template.

From our previous example of `page.html` file, notice the first line uses the `extends` tag:

```
{% extends "base.html" %}

{% block content %}
   This is the body of my press release.
{% endblock content %}
```

The `extends` tag takes a single argument specifying who the parent of this template is. In this example, `base.html` is the parent of `page.html`.

Here are a couple of important things to keep in mind about using the `extends` tag:

- In a child template, the `extends` tag should be the first tag in the file.
- The `extends` tag loads templates in the same way the function `get_template` does in the view. It's relative to the TEMPLATE_DIRS setting and can include subdirectories.
- If you try to extend a template that doesn't exist, you'll get an error.
- When writing your `endblock` tag, you don't have to put the name of the block, but it's a good idea to put it in for clarity.
- We specified a string of `"base.html"` as the argument to the tag, but you're not limited to strings. You can pass variables to your template to dynamically extend templates.

Because Django knows we will be using this template to extend another, it grabs all the blocks we defined and goes looking for the template we are going to extend. This is important because anything outside the block tags will be lost when the template is inherited into its parent!

For example, suppose we added an extra line to our `page.html` file before the content block:

```
{% extends "base.html" %}

Press Release

{% block content %}
This is the body of my press release.
{% endblock content %}
```

The words "Press Release" are not enclosed in any block tags. When the template engine parses this template file, these words will be lost because we didn't specify where we want them to go in the parent.

Adding inheritance to the press application

Let's incorporate these new concepts into our press application.

In the `mycompany/templates/press` directory, add a new file called `base.html` and add these lines:

```html
<html>
<head>
<title>Press Releases<title>
<style type="text/css">
body {
    text-align: center;
}
#container {
    margin: 0 auto;
    width: 70%;
    text-align: left;
}
.header {
    background-color: #000;
    color: #fff;
}
</style>
</head>
<body>
<div id="container">
<div class="header">
<h1>MyCompany Press Releases</h1>
</div>

{% block content %}{% endblock content %}

</div>
</body>
</html>
```

This file will serve as the parent template and acts like a shell that we will put content into.

Edit the `mycompany/templates/press/detail.html` file, replacing the contents with these lines:

```html
{% extends "press/base.html" %}

{% block content %}

<h2>{{ press.title }}</h2>
<p>
```

```
Author: {{ press.author }}<br/>
Date: {{ press.pub_date }}<br/>
</p>
<p>
{{ press.body }}
</p>

{% endblock content %}
```

What we have done is taken our press release detail template and broken it into pieces. The markup that controlled the layout of the page was put into the `base.html` file, and the handling of the "guts" of the page where the press release details are rendered was kept in `detail.html` and surrounded with a `block` tag.

Point your browser to the URL `http://localhost:8000/press/detail/1/`, and you should see something like the following:

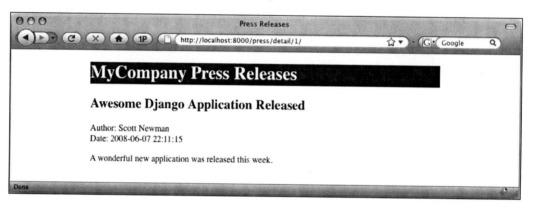

We've used a block tag called `content` in our child template and a corresponding block tag in our parent template to put the press release details into the base template. We still have a generic title "Press Releases" that should be replaced with the title of the press release. To do this, we need to create a second block in our parent template.

Using multiple block tags

To get our title into the parent template, we'll create a second block tag called `title` that our child templates can use to pass a page title. You can define multiple blocks inside a template as long as they have different names.

In the `mycompany/templates/press/detail.html` file, add a new block tag called `title` to the top, underneath the `extends` tag and before the `block content` tag:

```
{% extends "press/base.html" %}

{% block title %}
  {{ press.title }}
{% endblock title %}
```

In the `mycompany/templates/press/base.html` file, edit the `<title>` tag to use our new block:

```
<title>{% block title %}{% endblock title %}<title>
```

Point your browser to the URL `http://localhost:8000/press/detail/1/`, and you should see the title of the press release in the browser window's title bar.

Adding template inheritance to our press release list

Since we've already split up our press release detail template, we should do the same to our press release list page.

Edit the `mycompany/templates/press/list.html` file, replacing the contents with these lines:

```
{% extends "press/base.html" %}

{% block title %}
  All Press Releases
{% endblock title %}

{% block content %}

<h2>All Press Releases</h2>

<ul>
  {% for press in press_list %}
    <li>
      <a href="/press/release/detail/{{ press.id }}/">
      {{ press.title }}</a>
    </li>
  {% endfor %}
</ul>

{% endblock content %}
```

Point your browser to the URL `http://localhost:8000/press/list/` and you should see something similar to this:

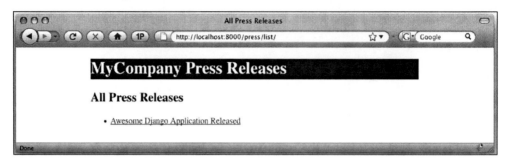

By splitting our templates into pieces, we're able to reuse the shell of the page in multiple press release pages, saving us work if we decide later to change the look of the page.

Inheriting from multiple child templates

We've taken the press release section of our project and defined a base template that acts as a parent template, and two child templates that can extend the base template. In a real-world project, we'd take this one step further and create another parent template for use site-wide. With this setup, we'd have a site-wide base template, a section-wide base template, and child templates that inherit from the section-wide base.

Here's an illustration of how that would look:

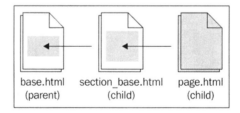

Let's add this three-level setup to our project. We'll have to make three changes: add a site base template, change the section base template to extend the site base, and move site-wide code from the section base to the site base.

In the `mycompany/templates` directory, add a new file called `site_base.html`, adding the following lines:

```
<html>
<head>
<title>{% block title %}{% endblock title %}<title>
```

```
<style type="text/css">
body {
    text-align: center;
}
#container {
    margin: 0 auto;
    width: 70%;
    text-align: left;
}
.header {
    background-color: #000;
    color: #fff;
}
</style>
</head>
<body>
<div id="container">
<div class="header">
<h1>
{% block header %}{% endblock header %}
</h1>
</div>

{% block site_content %}{% endblock site_content %}

</div>
</body>
</html>
```

Notice that we've added a new block called header for the header text for the page and changed the name of the main block in the body to site_content.

Edit the mycompany/templates/press/base.html file, replacing the contents with these lines:

```
{% extends "site_base.html" %}

{% block header %}
MyCompany Press Releases
{% endblock header %}

{% block site_content %}

{% block content %}{% endblock %}

<hr/>
For questions regarding press releases, please contact John Doe at
555-5555.

{% endblock site_content %}
```

Point your browser to the URL `http://localhost:8000/press/list/` and it should look something like this:

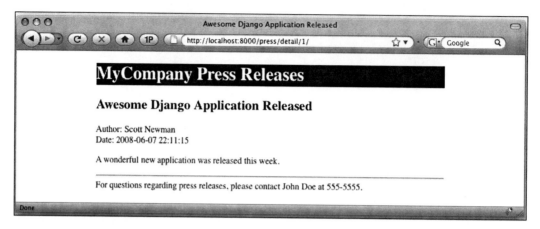

We've added a section-specific footer to our press release pages (call John Doe) by putting it inside the `site_content` block. In our `detail.html` template, the body of the press release is put into a block called `content`, which is then put into the block called `site_content` in `base.html`, its parent template.

In our `detail.html` template, we defined a block called `title` to hold our page title. Notice that we didn't do anything with it in `base.html`. Instead, it's carried all the way to our `site_base.html` file. It's perfectly acceptable to define blocks that "jump" up the inheritance tree.

Appending to blocks

Up to this point, we've been filling blocks with content from child templates. What if you wanted to leave any default content in that block and add to it the contents of the child template?

To do this, we use a special variable called `{{ block.super }}`. This variable holds whatever the block contains before being overwritten by the block from a child template.

In our `mycompany/templates/site_base.html` file, let's add a default page title:

```
<title>{% block title %}MyCompany{% endblock title %}</title>
```

We want to leave the word "MyCompany" in the title of the page and append more text to it, and so we use the `{{ block.super }}` variable in our child template.

Edit the contents of the `title` block in the `mycompany/templates/press/detail.html` file:

```
{% block title %}
{{ block.super }}: {{ press.title }}
{% endblock title %}
```

When the page is rendered, the page title will be output with "`MyCompany:`" in front of the page title.

Template strategy

There is no "magic number" or "correct" number of template files to have in your site. Every project's needs are different; some sites will have just a couple of templates, others may have dozens.

A good rule of thumb is that if you are repeating any part of your template on more than one or two pages, it's a good candidate to be put in its own file. This will save you time and effort down the line when you have to maintain these files by only having to make a change in one place.

With some planning, you can make your templates very flexible by creating blocks in your templates that you can use in child templates when the need arises.

Creating content placeholders

One thing you'll probably want to do in your templates is create placeholders for JavaScript and CSS that can be supplied by your child templates.

 When you define a block in a parent template, you are not required to use it in a child template. If you don't, the template engine will just return an empty block.

Extra JS

By defining an `extra_js` block, you can add additional page-specific JavaScript in a child template. In your `mycompany/templates/site_base.html` file, add the highlighted lines:

```
<html>
<head>
<title>{% block title %}MyCompany{% endblock title %}<title>
<style type="text/css">
body {
```

```
        text-align: center;
    }
    #container {
        margin: 0 auto;
        width: 70%;
        text-align: left;
    }
    .header {
        background-color: #000;
        color: #fff;
    }
    </style>
    <script>
    {% block extra_js %}{% endblock extra_js %}
    </script>
    </head>
```

Extra style

Like the `extra_js` block we created above, let's add an `extra_style` block. If you have CSS that isn't a part of a library used on every page, you can specify it in a child template. In your `mycompany/templates/site_base.html` file, add the highlighted line:

```
    <html>
    <head>
    <title>{% block title %}MyCompany{% endblock title %}<title>
    <style type="text/css">
    body {
        text-align: center;
    }
    #container {
        margin: 0 auto;
        width: 70%;
        text-align: left;
    }
    .header {
        background-color: #000;
        color: #fff;
    }
    {% block extra_style %}{% endblock %}
    </style>
    <script>
    {% block extra_js %}{% endblock extra_js %}
    </script>
    </head>
```

Extra head content

Finally, create an `extra_head` block before the closing `</head>` tag. This will give you the flexibility to inject any additional markup you might need in the head of the document, such as `meta` or `script` tags and blocks. In your `mycompany/templates/site_base.html` file, add the highlighted line above the closing `</head>` tag:

```
{% block extra_head %}{% endblock %}
</head>
```

Extra body tag attributes

This clever block can save you headache if you need to run a specific JavaScript function on the page load or unload. In your `mycompany/templates/site_base.html` file, edit the `body` tag to look like this:

```
<body {% spaceless %}
        {% block extra_body %}{% endblock extra_body %}
      {% endspaceless %}>
```

 You don't need to put in line breaks; this was done to fit the format here. The `spaceless` tag is important as it will remove any line breaks you might accidentally introduce into the tag. Some web browsers choke when your `body` tag has line breaks in it.

For example, if you're using a Google map on one of your pages and need to make sure a function is called when the body loads, you can specify it like this in a template:

```
{% block extra_body %}
 onload="initialize()" onunload="GUnload()"
{% endblock extra_body %}
```

When your page is rendered, it will look like this:

```
<body onload="initialize()" onunload="GUnload()">
```

With these extra blocks defined, you can add markup, script, and CSS as needed to your `site_base.html` template. Here's how it looks when completed:

```
<html>
<head>
<title>{% block title %}MyCompany{% endblock title %}<title>
<style type="text/css">
body {
    text-align: center;
```

```
}
#container {
    margin: 0 auto;
    width: 70%;
    text-align: left;
}
.header {
    background-color: #000;
    color: #fff;
}
{% block extra_style %}{% endblock %}
</style>
<script>
{% block extra_js %}{% endblock extra_js %}
</script>
{% block extra_head %}{% endblock %}
</head>
<body {% spaceless %}
        {% block extra_body %}{% endblock extra_body %}
    {% endspaceless %}>

<div id="container">
```

Using include files

Though we saw the limitations of using `include` files earlier in this chapter, there
are times when they can be useful. If you have a piece of content that you need to
include in some child templates, it may not make sense to create extra parent/child
relationships just to drop in this content. Let's look at two options that Django
provides us to easily include content.

Using include

To take the contents of a template file and put it into another template, use the
`include` tag. Pass the tag a template file name to include just like you did with the
`extends` tag:

```
{% include "menu.html" %}
```

In this hypothetical example, the `menu.html` file will be loaded the same way other
templates are loaded by the template engine. The location of the file is relative to the
`TEMPLATE_DIRS` setting, and the file is parsed by the template engine using the same
context variables as the template that called it.

Because the `include` files are also rendered with the context, you can use template tags and variables in them.

If you attempt to include a file that does not exist, Django will raise a `TemplateDoesNotExist error`.

Using SSI

Django offers an interesting alternative to the `include` tag, the `ssi` tag. (**SSI** stands for **Server Side Include**, something that was commonly used in the early days of web development.) At first glance, the `ssi` and `include` tags seem identical, but there is a critical difference. The `ssi` tag takes a full filesystem path to the file and doesn't work in conjunction with your `TEMPLATE_DIRS` setting.

The `include` tag uses the same syntax as `extends`. The file location is relative to the `TEMPLATE_DIRS` setting in your `settings.py` file. The `ssi` tag allows you to include any file from the filesystem, regardless of your `TEMPLATE_DIRS` setting.

```
{% ssi /home/scott/bio.html %}
```

 Don't put quotes around the argument to the `ssi` tag. If you do, it won't find the file and will return an error message into your template. It's odd and seems inconsistent with the rest of Django, but that's how it works as version 1.0. Perhaps it will change in the future versions.

Unlike the `include` tag, the `ssi` tag does not parse the contents of the included file by default. If you want to use variables in the file, you'll need to specify `parsed` in the call:

```
{% ssi /home/scott/bio.html parsed %}
```

If you don't provide the `parsed` argument and have variables in the file, they will be treated as text and not replaced. (You'll end up with a markup such as `{{ variable }}` in your output.)

In order to use the `ssi` tag, you have to specify an `ALLOWED_INCLUDE_ROOTS` variable in your `settings.py` file:

```
ALLOWED_INCLUDE_ROOTS = (
    "/some/path/on/your/server/",
)
```

If you try to use `ssi` to include a file in a directory that you haven't given permission to with `ALLOWED_INCLUDE_ROOTS`, you'll see this error message displayed in the output of your template when rendered:

[Didn't have permission to include file]

This error is different than the error when you try to include an invalid file. As we saw with `include`, the engine will raise an error and your page will not display. With `ssi`, you get this permission error written out in text as part of your template.

Summary

In this chapter, we looked at how the Django template system gets configured and how template inheritance works.

Specifically, we looked at the following:

- The three template loader types: the `filesystem` loader, the `app_directories` loader, and the `eggs` loader
- How the `filesystem` and `app_directories` loaders are configured, how they work, and how they can be configured to work together
- How Django calls templates for 404 and 500 errors
- The order in which Django looks for templates when multiple loader types are used
- The difference between including and extending templates
- How template inheritance works
- How to use `block` tags in templates
- Using `block.super` to append to blocks
- Creating reusable site elements with inheritance and includes
- Creating flexible templates by defining placeholder blocks in our parent templates
- How to use the `include` and `ssi` tags

In the next chapter, we will look at serving multiple templates from a single project.

6

Serving Multiple Templates

There are times when we will need to serve the same content in multiple ways whether it's displaying a printable version of a page, creating festive themes for holidays or promotions, or using a different set of templates for mobile devices.

There are a number of approaches to these tasks, and no one is "right". As we will see, the best choice depends on the circumstances specific to your site and users.

In this chapter we will:

- Consider the different approaches to tailoring output
- Explore the challenges of serving content to mobile devices
- Create printer-friendly output via URL parameters
- Easily create site themes by overriding template files
- Use a second domain name to serve mobile templates
- Automatically redirect mobile users to an alternative URL

Considering the different approaches

Though there are different approaches that can be taken to serve content in multiple formats, the best solution will be specific to your circumstances and implementation.

Almost any approach you take will have maintenance overhead. You'll have multiple places to update when things change. As copies of your template files proliferate, a simple text change can become a large task.

Some of the cases we'll look at don't require much consideration. Serving a printable version of a page, for example, is straightforward and easily accomplished. Putting a pumpkin in your site header at Halloween or using a heart background around Valentine's Day can make your site seem timely and relevant, especially if you are in a seasonal business.

Other techniques, such as serving different templates to different browsers, devices, or user-agents might create serious debate among content authors. Since serving content to mobile devices is becoming a new standard of doing business, we'll make it the focus of this chapter.

Serving mobile devices

The Mobile Web will remind some old timers (like me!) of the early days of web design where we'd create different sites for Netscape and Internet Explorer. Hopefully, we take lessons from those days as we go forward and don't repeat our mistakes. Though we're not as apt to serve wholly different templates to different desktop browsers as we once were, the mobile device arena creates special challenges that require careful attention.

One way to serve both desktop and mobile devices is a one-size-fits-all approach. Through carefully structured and semantically correct XHTML markup and CSS selectors identified to be applied to handheld output, you can do a reasonable job of making your content fit a variety of contexts and devices.

However, this method has a couple of serious shortcomings. First, it does not take into account the limitations of devices for rich media presentation with Flash, JavaScript, DHTML, and AJAX as they are largely unsupported on all but the highest-end devices. If your site depends on any of these technologies, your users can get frustrated when trying to experience it on a mobile device.

Also, it doesn't address the varying levels of CSS support by different mobile devices. What looks perfect on one device might look passable on another and completely unusable on a third because only some of the CSS rules were applied properly. It also does not take into account the potentially high bandwidth costs for large markup files and CSS for users who pay by the amount of data transferred. For example, putting `display: none` on an image doesn't stop a mobile device from downloading the file. It only prevents it from being shown.

Finally, this approach doesn't tailor the experience to the user's circumstances. Users tend to be goal-oriented and have specific actions in mind when using the mobile web, and content designers should recognize that simply recreating the desktop experience on a smaller screen might not solve their needs. Limiting the information to what a mobile user is looking for and designing a simplified navigation can provide a better user experience.

Adapting content

You know your users best, and it is up to you to decide the best way to serve them. You may decide to pass on the one-size-fits-all approach and serve a separate mobile experience through content adaptation.

The W3C's Mobile Web Initiative best practices guidelines suggest giving users the flexibility and freedom to choose their experience, and provide links between the desktop and mobile templates so that they can navigate between the two. It is generally not recommended to automatically redirect users on mobile devices to a mobile site unless you give them a way to access the full site.

The dark side to this kind of content adaptation is that you will have a second set of template files to keep updated when you make site changes. It can also cause your visitors to search through different bookmarks to find the content they have saved.

Before we get into multiple sites, let's start with some examples of showing alternative templates on our current site.

Setting up our example

In Chapter 2, we worked with the Press Release application, configuring it to work with both regular and generic views. Let's continue to use this application and modify it to serve data in a few different formats. Also, at the end of Chapter 2 we set up our application to serve the detail page with a generic view, saving us from having to write a view to serve the detail of a press release.

Because we want to customize the output of our detail page based on the presence of a variable in the URL, we're going to use our view function again instead of the generic view. If you didn't delete it, the view function should still be in your `mycompany/press/views.py` file. (It's included below in case you deleted it.)

Edit your `mycompany/press/urls.py` file, removing the generic view for the press release detail page and inserting the highlighted line as shown:

```
urlpatterns = patterns('',
    (r'detail/(?P<pid>\d+)/$',
        'mycompany.press.views.detail'),
    (r'list/$','django.views.generic.list_detail.object_list',
        press_list_dict),
    (r'latest/$','mycompany.press.views.latest'),
    (r'$','django.views.generic.simple.redirect_to',
        {'url': '/press/list/'})
)
```

In your `mycompany/press/views.py` file, your detail view should look like this:

```
def detail(request, pid):
    '''
    Accepts a press release ID and returns the detail page
    '''
    p = get_object_or_404(PressRelease, id=pid)
    t = loader.get_template('press/detail.html')
    c = Context({'press': p})
    return HttpResponse(t.render(c))
```

Let's jazz up our template a little more for the press release detail by adding some CSS to it. In `mycompany/templates/press/detail.html`, edit the file to look like this:

```
<html>
<head>
<title>{{ press.title }}</title>
<style type="text/css">
body {
    text-align: center;
}
#container {
    margin: 0 auto;
    width: 70%;
    text-align: left;
}
.header {
    background-color: #000;
    color: #fff;
}
</style>
</head>
<body>
<div id="container">
<div class="header">
<h1>MyCompany Press Releases</h1>
</div>
<div>
<h2>{{ press.title }}</h2>
<p>
Author: {{ press.author }}<br/>
Date: {{ press.pub_date }}<br/>
</p>
<p>
{{ press.body }}
</p>
</div>
</body>
</html>
```

Start your development server and point your browser to the URL
`http://localhost:8000/press/detail/1/`. You should see something
like this, depending on what you entered when you originally created your
press release:

If your press release detail page is serving correctly, you're ready to continue.

You may be wondering why we originally created the detail page and
used a regular view, then changed it to a generic view, and now are
changing it back again. Don't get frustrated—this is all a part of learning!

Remember that we said the generic views can save us development time,
but sometimes you'll need to use a regular view because you're doing
something in a way that requires a view function customized to the task
at hand.

The exercise we're about to do is one of those circumstances, and after
going through the exercise, you'll have a better idea of when to use one
type of view over another.

Serving printable pages

One of the easiest approaches we will look at is serving an alternative version of a
page based on the presence of a variable in the URL (aka a URL parameter). To serve
a printable version of an article, for example, we can add `?printable` to the end of
the URL.

To make it work, we'll add an extra step in our view to check the URL for this
variable. If it exists, we'll load up a printer-friendly template file. If it doesn't exist,
we'll load the normal template file.

Start by editing the highlighted lines to the `detail` function in the `mycompany/press/views.py` file:

```
def detail(request, pid):
    '''
    Accepts a press release ID and returns the detail page
    '''
    p = get_object_or_404(PressRelease, id=pid)

    if request.GET.has_key('printable'):
        template_file = 'press/detail_printable.html'
    else:
        template_file = 'press/detail.html'

    t = loader.get_template(template_file)
    c = Context({'press': p})
    return HttpResponse(t.render(c))
```

We're looking at the `request.GET` object to see if a query string parameter of `printable` was present in the current request. If it was, we load the `press/detail_printable.html` file. If not, we load the `press/detail.html` file. We've also changed the `loader.get_template` function to look for the `template_file` variable.

To test our changes, we'll need to create a simple version of our template that only has minimal formatting. Create a new file called `detail_printable.html` in the `mycompany/templates/press/` directory and add these lines into it:

```
<html>
<head>
<title>{{ press.title }}</title>
</head>
<body>
<h1>{{ press.title }}</h1>
<p>
Author: {{ press.author }}<br/>
Date: {{ press.pub_date }}<br/>
</p>
<p>
{{ press.body }}
</p>
</body>
</html>
```

Now that we have both regular and printable templates, let's test our view. Point your browser to the URL `http://localhost:8000/press/detail/1/`, and you should see our original template as it was before. Change the URL to `http://localhost:8000/press/detail/1/?printable` and you should see our new printable template:

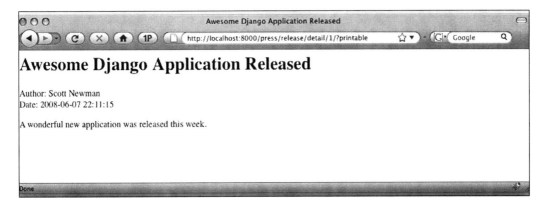

Creating site themes

Depending on the audience and focus of your site, you may want to temporarily change the look of your site for a season or holiday such as Halloween or Valentine's Day. This is easily accomplished by leveraging the power of the TEMPLATE_DIRS configuration setting.

You will recall from an earlier chapter that the TEMPLATE_DIRS variable in the `settings.py` file allows you to specify the location of the templates for your site. One thing about which we didn't go into detail was that TEMPLATE_DIRS allows you to specify multiple locations for your template files.

When you specify multiple paths for your template files, Django will look for a requested template file in the first path, and if it doesn't find it, it will keep searching through the remaining paths until the file is located.

We can use this to our advantage by adding an `override` directory as the first element of the TEMPLATE_DIRS value. When we want to override a template with a special themed one, we'll add the file to the `override` directory. The next time the template loader tries to load the template, it will find it in the `override` directory and serve it.

For example, let's say we want to override our press release page from the previous example. Recall that the view loaded the template like this (from `mycompany/press/views.py`):

```
template_file = 'press/detail.html'
t = loader.get_template(template_file)
```

When the template engine loads the `press/detail.html` template file, it gets it from the `mycompany/templates/` directory as specified in the `mycompany/settings.py` file:

```
TEMPLATE_DIRS = (
    '/projects/mycompany/templates/',
)
```

If we add an additional directory to our `TEMPLATE_DIRS` setting, Django will look in the new directory first:

```
TEMPLATE_DIRS = (
    '/projects/mycompany/templates/override/',
    '/projects/mycompany/templates/',
)
```

Now when the template is loaded, it will first check for the file `/projects/mycompany/templates/override/press/detail.html`. If that file doesn't exist, it will go on to the next directory and look for the file in `/projects/mycompany/templates/press/detail.html`.

 If you're using Windows, use the Windows-style file path `c:/projects/mycompany/templates/` for these examples.

Therein lies the beauty. If we want to override our press release template, we simply drop an alternative version with the same file name into the `override` directory. When we're done using it, we just remove it from the `override` directory and the original version will be served (or rename the file in the override directory to something other than `detail.html`).

 If you're concerned about the performance overhead of having a nearly empty `override` directory that is constantly checked for the existence of template files, we'll look at caching techniques in a later chapter as a potential solution for this problem.

Testing the template overrides

Let's create a template override to test the concept we just learned. In your `mycompany/settings.py` file, edit the `TEMPLATE_DIRS` setting to look like this:

```
TEMPLATE_DIRS = (
    '/projects/mycompany/templates/override/',
    '/projects/mycompany/templates/',
)
```

Create a directory called `override` at `mycompany/templates/` and another directory underneath that called `press`. You should now have these directories:

```
/projects/mycompany/templates/override/
/projects/mycompany/templates/override/press/
```

Create a new file called `detail.html` in `mycompany/templates/override/press/` and add these lines to the file:

```
<html>
<head>
<title>{{ press.title }}</title>
</head>
<body>
<h1>Happy Holidays</h1>
<h2>{{ press.title }}</h2>
<p>
Author: {{ press.author }}<br/>
Date: {{ press.pub_date }}<br/>
</p>
<p>
{{ press.body }}
</p>
</body>
</html>
```

You'll probably notice that this is just our printable detail template with an extra "Happy Holidays" line added to the top of it.

Point your browser to the URL `http://localhost:8000/press/detail/1/` and you should see something like this:

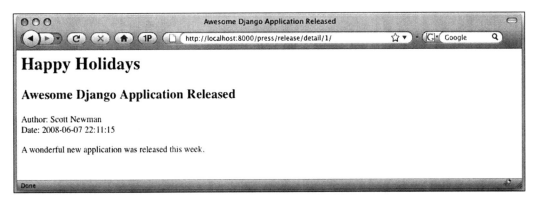

By creating a new press release detail template and dropping it in the `override` directory, we caused Django to automatically pick up the new template and serve it without us having to change the view. To change it back, you can simply remove the file from the `override` directory (or rename it).

One other thing to notice is that if you add `?printable` to the end of the URL, it still serves the printable version of the file we created earlier.

Delete the `mycompany/templates/override/` directory and any files in it as we won't need them again.

Serving different templates by domain name

An increasingly common need for web applications is to serve a set of alternative templates for mobile devices. A common way to serve this alternative view of your site is to use a different domain name, such as `mobile.mydomain.com`, `m.mydomain.com` or `mydomain.mobi`.

Django makes it very easy to serve a secondary domain name from the same base project. When you configure your web server to serve your Django site, you tell it what settings file to use, so you can create a second settings file in the same directory and give it a different value for the `TEMPLATE_DIRS` setting.

For example, your main site would point to `mycompany/settings.py` and have a `TEMPLATE_DIRS` setting like this:

```
TEMPLATE_DIRS = (
    '/projects/mycompany/templates/',
)
```

Your mobile site would point to `mycompany/settings_mobile.py` with a `TEMPLATE_DIRS` setting like this:

```
TEMPLATE_DIRS = (
    '/projects/mycompany/templates/mobile/',
)
```

This technique gets even better when you realize that you don't have to completely duplicate your `settings.py` file when creating `settings_mobile.py`. Because the only thing we need to change between the two files is the `TEMPLATE_DIRS` value, the only lines you need to put in your `settings_mobile.py` file are these:

```
from settings import *
TEMPLATE_DIRS = (
    '/projects/mycompany/templates/mobile/',
)
```

The first line imports all the existing values from the mycompany/settings.py file. The second line overrides the value of TEMPLATE_DIRS with our new directory. This technique has the added benefit that changes to the settings.py file don't have to be duplicated into settings_mobile.py. They will be automatically picked up.

Serving different sites with the development web server

We can test how this works by using the development web server that we've been using all along and specifying which settings file to use. (You can also make your production web server, such as Apache or lighttpd do this. You'll find configuration information in Django's online documentation.) We'll start two instances of the development server on different ports to simulate the real-world example of using two different domains.

Step 1: Cloning the settings File

Create a new file in your mycompany directory called settings_mobile.py. In that file, insert these lines:

```
from settings import *
TEMPLATE_DIRS = (
    '/projects/mycompany/templates/mobile/',
)
```

Because this file exists in the same directory as settings.py, it's able to use a simple import statement to bring in all its values.

Step 2: Create a mobile template

We won't go into the details of creating templates that are friendly to mobile web browsers, as there is plenty of information available online on this. (If you're interested, dev.mobi is an excellent resource for information on that subject as well as *Mobile Web Development* by Nirav Mehta, printed by Packt Publishing.)

To test our setup, we'll create a different template so that we can see that it served properly. Create a new directory in mycompany/templates/ called mobile. Create a press directory in the mycompany/templates/mobile/ directory.

You should now have these directories:

```
mycompany/templates/press/
mycompany/templates/mobile/press/
```

Create a new file called `detail.html` in your `mycompany/templates/mobile/`
`press/` directory and add these lines:

```html
<html>
<head>
<title>{{ press.title }}</title>
</head>
<body>
<h1>MyCompany Mobile</h1>
<h2>{{ press.title }}</h2>
<p>
Author: {{ press.author }}<br/>
Date: {{ press.pub_date }}<br/>
</p>
<p>
{{ press.body }}
</p>
</body>
</html>
```

Step 3: Configuring the development web server

When using the development web server, it's possible to tell it what settings file to
run against by passing a command-line argument:

```
$ manage.py runserver --settings=settings_mobile
```

Using two separate terminal windows, run two different instances of the web server
at two different ports so that we can test the differences:

```
$ manage.py runserver 8000 --settings=settings
```

```
$ manage.py runserver 8001 --settings=settings_mobile
```

If we point our web browser at the URL `http://localhost:8000/press/`
`detail/1/`, we'll get the regular version of our press release. If we use the URL
`http://localhost:8001/press/detail/1/`, we'll get the new mobile version of
the site like this:

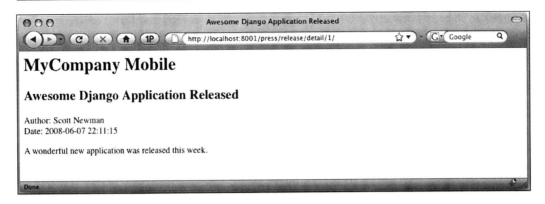

 I was introduced to this method by Matt Croydon's blog at `postneo.com`. He agreed to let me share it in this chapter. Thanks, Matt!

Redirecting users to the mobile site (optional)

I saved this section for last because it's entirely optional and uses some advanced concepts. You can consider it as an extra credit exercise. None of the examples in the rest of the book rely on it, so you can safely skip it if you want.

Now that we have a second site set up for mobile users, we may want to automatically redirect our users to it if we can tell they are using a mobile device.

 Caution: This technique isn't foolproof and could cause difficulties for some of your users who want to be able to choose their mobile experience. We'll code a way with which they can get back to the main site, but consider this when deciding if you want to use the technique.

Detecting mobile devices

The `HTTP_USER_AGENT` is the key piece of information we will use to determine how the user is accessing the site. It's a string containing the identity of the browser being used; consider it the "fingerprint" of the browser. In Django, the user agent string is available from the key `request.META['HTTP_USER_AGENT']`.

Here's the user agent from iPhone (There is no line break, it's one long, continued line.):

```
Mozilla/5.0 (iPhone; U; CPU like Mac OS X; en) AppleWebKit/420+
(KHTML, like Gecko) Version/3.0 Mobile/1A543a Safari/419.3
```

Notice that the string is full of version numbers. If you try to match on these strings directly, you could end up with hundreds or thousands of strings to check against, as new versions are released on different platforms. Inside the string, however, are two strings that we might use to give us a clue whether this is a mobile device, `Mobile` and `iPhone`.

Instead of seeing if the current user agent is equal to this string, we'll use regular expressions to look inside the string for patterns we know match common mobile user agents.

Here's a Python snippet from the interactive shell to illustrate the point:

```
>>> import re
>>> user_agent = '''Mozilla/5.0 (iPhone; U; CPU like Mac OS X; en)
AppleWebKit/420+ (KHTML, like Gecko) Version/3.0 Mobile/1A543a
Safari/419.3'''
>>> re.search('iPhone', user_agent)
<_sre.SRE_Match object at 0x736b0>
```

When we searched for the term `iPhone` inside of the `user_agent` string, we found a match. We can use this kind of test to determine if the request is coming from a mobile device. We could check this in each of our views, but that would require a lot of redundant code. Instead, we'll write it into a piece of Django middleware that will run before each request is processed.

 Regular expressions can be tricky to work with, and you may want to read up on how they work before diving in. They can be incredibly powerful, so it's probably time well spent!

Writing the middleware

You'll recall from a previous chapter that middleware functions allow you to "tap in" or inject functions into the request and response cycle. We'll use a `process_request` middleware function to check for a mobile device before any views are executed.

The first thing we'll need to do is create a directory under our project in which to put our middleware file. Create a new directory under the existing `mycompany` directory called `middleware`. Inside the new directory, we'll create two files:

- `mycompany/middleware/__init__.py`
- `mycompany/middleware/mobile_redirect.py`

The first file, __init__.py, is just a blank file that Python needs for its importing process. Don't worry too much about it; just create it as a blank file. The second file, mobile_redirect.py, will contain the logic to do our redirection.

Here's the first pass at our code. Enter these lines in mobile_redirect.py:

```
from django.http import HttpResponseRedirect
import re

mobile_url = 'http://localhost:8001/'

agents_list = [
    'Nokia','\bMOT','^LGE?\b','SonyEricsson',
    'Ericsson','BlackBerry','DoCoMo','Symbian',
    'Windows\ CE','NetFront','Klondike','PalmOS',
    'PalmSource','portalmm','S[CG]H-','\bSAGEM',
    'SEC-','jBrowser-WAP','Mitsu','Panasonic-',
    'SAMSUNG-','Samsung-','Sendo','SHARP-',
    'Vodaphone','BenQ','iPAQ','AvantGo',
    'Go.Web','Sanyo-','AUDIOVOX','PG-',
    'CDM[-\d]','^KDDI-','^SIE-','TSM[-\d]',
    '^KWC-','WAP','^KGT [NC]','iPhone',
]

def is_mobile(user_agent):
    for agent in agents_list:
        if re.search(agent, user_agent):
            return True
    return False

class MobileRedirect(object):
    def process_request(self, request):
        if is_mobile(request.META['HTTP_USER_AGENT']):
            return HttpResponseRedirect(mobile_url)
        else:
            pass
        return None
```

Starting at the bottom, we've created a generic object called MobileRedirect that has a process_request method. (Django's middleware system requires us to set it up this way.)

We're calling a function is_mobile_device that takes the user agent as an argument, determines if it matches against a list of known mobile agents, and returns a Boolean True or False. If it matched, we redirect the user to our mobile site. If not, the middleware will return None and Django will continue.

The `is_mobile_device` function iterates through a list of regular expression patterns and looks for a match. Notice that the `user_agents` list contains regular expression patterns just like the one we worked with a minute ago. You'll see some regular expression syntax such as \b and \d that match the pattern as a word (not a piece in the middle of a string) and match digits, respectively.

Checking only once

There are a couple of potential downsides to this technique. First, most visitors to your site will probably not have browsers with user agent strings that match against this list and get redirected to your mobile site. Running this piece of middleware on every request is a waste of resources and could negatively impact performance.

Second, it doesn't give your user the option of viewing your desktop site on his/her mobile device as they are automatically redirected. Users with advanced mobile browsers such as the iPhone may want to use your full site. Every time they try to access the full site, they will get redirected to the mobile site.

The easiest way to get around both these problems is to use a session variable to record that we have already performed the user agent check. Sessions are turned on by default in Django, so we'll just add a couple lines:

```
class MobileRedirect(object):
    def process_request(self, request):
        if not request.session.get('checked_ua', False):
            if is_mobile(request.META['HTTP_USER_AGENT']):
                request.session['checked_ua'] = True
                return HttpResponseRedirect(mobile_url)
            else:
                # Make sure it doesn't try this again
                request.session['checked_ua'] = True
        return None
```

Here we've added a session variable `checked_ua` that we can check before we run the `is_mobile_device` function. If the session variable evaluates to `True`, we skip over the processing and Django continues on its way.

If it's not `True`, we check the user agent and use the `checked_ua` variable to record that we've done the processing. This solves our second problem, which we identified: If the user goes back to our full site, they won't get redirected again because the session variable will indicate that the check was already performed. We'll know they were redirected and they came back, so they probably don't want to be redirected again!

Django's session framework requires cookies to work properly. Most modern mobile browsers support cookies, so this technique should work well. If the mobile browser doesn't support cookies or they are disabled, the user will not be able to get back to your full site because the session won't exist.

Installing the middleware

The last thing we need to do is add our function to the MIDDLEWARE_CLASSES setting inside our mycompany/settings.py file. We also need to override the setting inside of our mobile_settings.py file, otherwise it will keep trying to redirect to itself!

In your mycompany/settings.py file, add the highlighted line to the MIDDLEWARE_CLASSES setting:

```
MIDDLEWARE_CLASSES = (
    'django.middleware.common.CommonMiddleware',
    'django.contrib.sessions.middleware.SessionMiddleware',
    'middleware.mobile_redirect.MobileRedirect',
    'django.contrib.auth.middleware.AuthenticationMiddleware',
)
```

Notice that we put the mobile redirect middleware after the session middleware. If we don't, we will not be able to write the session variable that we need. The order matters!

Finally, in our settings_mobile.py file, add the MIDDLEWARE_CLASSES setting without the mobile redirect:

```
MIDDLEWARE_CLASSES = (
    'django.middleware.common.CommonMiddleware',
    'django.contrib.sessions.middleware.SessionMiddleware',
    'django.contrib.auth.middleware.AuthenticationMiddleware',
)
```

You may be wondering why we did this with a session variable instead of a cookie. In order to set cookies, we need to have access to the HTTP response object that is written, as that's where cookie writing happens. Since we don't have this object in the process_request middleware, we kept it simple by using session variables.

To test the middleware in your web browser, you'll need to change the browser's user agent string. An easy way to do this in the Firefox browser is to install a plug-in called the User Agent Switcher. This browser add-in allows your desktop web browser to masquerade as a different user agent.

 You can find the add-in at https://addons.mozilla.org/en-US/firefox/addon/59.

I installed the add-in in my Firefox application, and followed the directions provided to add a new user agent. I used these settings:

- Description: iPhone
- User Agent: Mozilla/5.0 (iPhone; U; CPU like Mac OS X; en)
- AppleWebKit/420+ (KHTML, like Gecko)
- Version/3.0
- Mobile/1A542a Safari/419.3

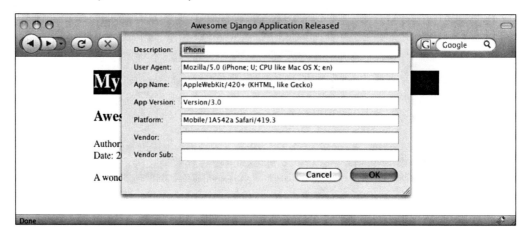

With these settings in place, I went up to Firefox's **Tools** menu, chose **User Agent Switcher**, and chose the new **iPhone** setting. With this setting, my browser tricks web servers into thinking it's an iPhone.

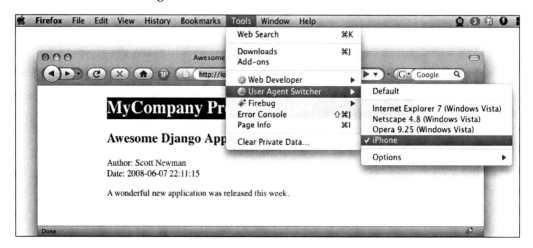

Browse to the URL `http://localhost:8000/`, and the middleware should immediately try to redirect you to `http://localhost:8001/`.

Summary

In this chapter, we've explored the topic of serving content with multiple templates. We looked at the different approaches available to serve content to mobile devices, including using basic templates and content adaptation.

We learned how to detect the presence of a URL parameter to dynamically choose the template loaded in a view, and how to use the TEMPLATE_DIRS setting to override a template on demand without having to change any code.

Finally, we leaned how to serve a second set of templates to a separate domain name by creating a settings file to override the default settings. We also explored a technique using middleware to redirect users to a different URL based on their browser's user agent string.

In the next chapter, we'll look at Custom Tags and Filters.

7
Custom Tags and Filters

Django ships with a number of built-in template tags and filters that fit the needs of most web-publishing situations. Filters are typically used to modify the output of a value in the template, and tags let you do just about anything you want.

At some point in your development, you may come across a situation or need that cannot be handled by the default template tags and filters. Luckily, Django provides a way to write our own extensions to the template engine by creating custom tags and filters.

In this chapter, we will:

- Review how the default template tags and filters are implemented
- Learn the syntax for writing our own template tags and filters
- Learn where to put our custom files in our project and how Django loads them
- Create and implement custom filters to format currency, remove profanities, and test if an item is in a list
- Create and implement custom tags to write output and introduce new variables into the context from within the template

Examining the built-in tags and filters

Before we start writing our own tags and filters, let's review how the built-in ones work. They are written and implemented in the same way that we will use to write our own, so looking at the code and its structure gives us some great examples as a starting point. You can browse the built-in tags and filters by looking at these files in the Django source code:

- `django/template/defaultfilters.py`
- `django/template/defaulttags.py`

Template filters

If you need to change the way a value outputs in a template, use a template filter. Typical filters modify string and number formats, add or remove characters, and so on. A filter is essentially a Python function that can take one or two arguments: the value it is working on, and an optional argument.

For example, the built-in filter `upper` transforms a template string to upper case:

```
{{ title|upper }}
```

Behind the scenes, it calls the `upper` function in `defaultfilters.py`:

```
def upper(value):
    """Converts a string into all uppercase."""
    return value.upper()
upper.is_safe = False
upper = stringfilter(upper)
```

In this example, the value of `title` is sent to the function `upper` as the argument `value`. The function returns the result of the string function `upper()`.

 Don't worry about `is_safe` and `stringfilter()` right now. We'll get to what they mean in a moment.

Template tags

Unlike filters, tags don't have to be passed any values or arguments and they can take multiple arguments if you need them to. If you want to perform more complex logic such as reordering lists, performing conditional logic, modifying context variables, etc., you'll want to use a template tag instead of a filter.

For example, if you want to output the current date or time and specify the format, you can use the built-in `now` tag:

```
The current year is {% now "Y" %}
```

Behind the scenes, it calls the `now` function in `defaulttags.py`:

```
def now(parser, token):
    """
    displays the date, formatted according to the given string.
    Uses the same format as PHP's date() function.
```

```
        See http://php.net/date for all the possible values.
        Sample usage:

        It is {% now "jS F Y H:i" %}
        """
        bits = token.contents.split('"')
        if len(bits) != 3:
            raise TemplateSyntaxError, "'now' statement takes one argument"
        format_string = bits[1]
        return NowNode(format_string)
    now = register.tag(now)
```

The template tag syntax is more complex than the filter syntax we saw earlier. Rather than overwhelm you with what it all means right now, let's just note that it has to figure out what the arguments to the tag were, make sure the tag got all the information it needed, and create a chunk of template called a `Node` that the template engine can then `render` as it would any other piece of template.

Writing your own template filters

Let's dive into writing our own filters. It can be hard to come up with a great example of a useful filter since the Django team has included default filters that serve most common needs, but we'll build three that can be helpful or can be later modified to fit your specific needs.

Setting up a test application

To experiment with tags and filters, we need to set up a test application that we can use as a sandbox to test our code. Instead of mucking up any apps that we have created in the previous chapters, we'll create a new project.

> Why not create custom tags and filters for our ongoing application? Well, Django has covered most of the common needs you'll have, so we need to reach deeper and create some samples that can be used for these more specific cases where a custom library needs to be created.

Create a new project called `customtags` in `/projects` and then create a `filtertest` application. (If you're using Windows, create it in `c:\projects`.)

In the `/projects` directory, run the `startproject` command:

```
$ django-admin.py startproject customtags
```

In the `/projects/customtags` directory, run the `startapp` command:

```
$ python manage.py startapp filtertest
```

In the `customtags/settings.py` file, replace the `TEMPLATE_DIRS` and `INSTALLED_APPS` tuples with these values:

```
TEMPLATE_DIRS = (
    '/projects/customtags/templates/',
)

INSTALLED_APPS = (
    'customtags.filtertest',
)
```

In the `customtags/urls.py` file, add these lines:

```
from django.conf.urls.defaults import *

urlpatterns = patterns('',
    (r'^filter/', 'customtags.filtertest.views.test'),
)
```

Create a `templates` directory under `/projects/customtags` and create a new file called `filter_test.html`, adding these lines:

```
<h1>These are test values</h1>
<p>A good Django app is worth: {{ myprice }}.</p>
<p>My thoughts on Django: {{ mythoughts }}</p>
<p>Words to describe Django: {{ mywords }}</p>
```

To keep things simple, we won't create any models for the `filtertest` application. Instead, we'll just manually pass some local variables in the view to our template context.

Finally, in `customtags/filtertest/views.py`, add these lines:

```
from django.http import HttpResponse
from django.template import Context, loader

def test(request):
    t = loader.get_template('filter_test.html')
    c = Context({
        'myprice': 10000,
        'mythoughts': 'Django is dang cool!',
```

```
            'mywords': ['great', 'awesome', 'fun'],
        })
        return HttpResponse(t.render(c))
```

Start the Django development server and point your browser to the URL `http://localhost:8000/filter/`. You should see the following page. If you don't, double-check that you have followed all the steps mentioned.

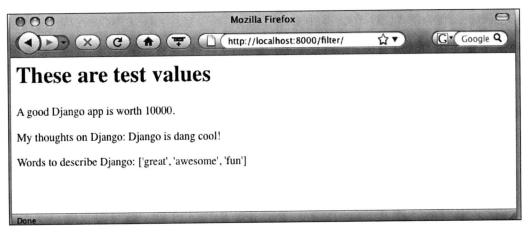

Now that we have something to work with, let's create some template filters to tweak the output of our three context variables.

Creating a home for our filter library

Before we can write our filters, we need to create a place to put them. By convention, Django requires us to create a directory called `templatetags` under an installed application and put our library files in it. Django scans for folders called `templatetags` when it initializes.

Create a directory at `customtags/filtertest/templatetags` and a file in it called `filtertest_extras.py`. This file is our template library file and can hold many filters that we create.

In the `customtags/filtertest/templatetags/filtertest_extras.py` file, add these lines:

```
from django import template

register = template.Library()
```

This code adds a variable called `register` to the module. It's required by the template engine to properly register the tags and filters in the file.

Finally, create a blank file called `__init__.py` in the directory `customtags/filtertest/templatetags`. Any directory that Python imports as a module needs to have an `__init__.py` file inside it, even if it's blank. Don't worry too much about this; it's just a Python convention that we need to follow.

Template filter syntax

Template filters are just Python functions that we can run from our templates. As you will recall from an earlier chapter, the Django template system limits our ability to call most functions directly in templates, but filters provide us a clean way to get a part of that functionality back.

The syntax of a filter looks like a typical Python function. The function takes two arguments:

1. The value of the template variable being modified
2. An optional filter argument (You cannot pass multiple arguments to a filter.)

Here's a simple example: If we were going to write a filter called `add_prefix` that added a string to the beginning of our value, we'd call it like this in the template:

```
{{ title|add_prefix:"zz" }}
```

In our hypothetical example, the `add_prefix` function would look like this:

```
def add_prefix(value, arg):
    return "%s_%s" % (arg, value)
register.filter(add_prefix)
```

The value of the `{{ title }}` context variable is the first argument to our `add_prefix` function. `zz` is the argument to the filter and is passed to our function as `arg`.

In order for Django to be able to call our filters, they must register themselves for use. We call the `register` function immediately after our filter function; do not put a line break between the function and the `register` call; it needs to "touch" (see the example above).

If you are using Python 2.4 or higher, you can call `register` using decorator syntax:

```
@register.filter
def add_prefix(value, arg):
    return "%s_%s" % (arg, value)
```

To find out what version of Python you are using, you can launch the Python interactive shell by typing `python` at the command line. The first line that comes up will have the Python version in it.

We won't be using the decorator syntax in this chapter, but you should know it's available if you want to use it. (Decorators are considered more "Pythonic", meaning "in the style that Python programmers prefer".)

Loading template libraries

Once we write our tags and filters, we need to load them in order to use them in our templates. When Django starts up, it scans all the installed applications for `templatetags` directories and records the template library files within them.

In your template, you call the `load` tag with the name of the file you want to load, minus the `.py` extension. To make it easier to remember its purpose, it can help to give your library file a descriptive name. We'll use `extras` in our filename to remember that they add extra functionality.

For example, our `customtags/filtertest/templatetags/filtertest_extras.py` file gets loaded in the template like this:

```
{% load filtertest_extras %}
```

Any custom tags and filters inside the `filtertest_extras` library are now available like the built-in ones. If you have a `uscurrency` filter defined in the `filtertest_extras.py` file, you can now use it with standard filter syntax:

```
The price is {{ myprice|uscurrency }}.
```

Since we don't have that, let's build it!

U.S. currency filter

This filter will take a number and put a dollar sign in front and two decimal places in the U.S. currency format, for example $99.88. To keep things simple, we won't be worrying about localizing currency values based on the user's country.

In our test application, we are passing the value `10000` in the context variable `myprice`. Let's build a filter that we can use like this to format the output with a dollar sign and two decimal places that will be called like this:

```
A good Django app is worth {{ myprice|uscurrency }}
```

In the `customtags/filtertest/templatetags/filtertest_extras.py` file, add the highlighted code block:

```
from django import template

register = template.Library()

def uscurrency(c):
    if c > 0:
        return '$%.2f' % c
    else:
        return '-$%.2f' % (-1*c)
register.filter(uscurrency)
```

In the `customtags/templates/filter_test.html` file, change the highlighted lines:

```
{% load filtertest_extras %}
<h1>These are test values</h1>
<p>
A good Django app is worth {{ myprice|uscurrency }}.
</p>
<p>My thoughts on Django: {{ mythoughts }}</p>
<p>Words to describe Django: {{ mywords }}</p>
```

We added the `{% load filtertag_extras %}` line to tell Django to load our `filtertest_extras.py` file. Remember that for this to work, the `filtertest_extras.py` file must be in a directory called `templatetags` under an installed application and there **must** be a blank file called `__init__.py` in that directory.

Point your browser to the URL `http://localhost:8000/filter/` and you should see this:

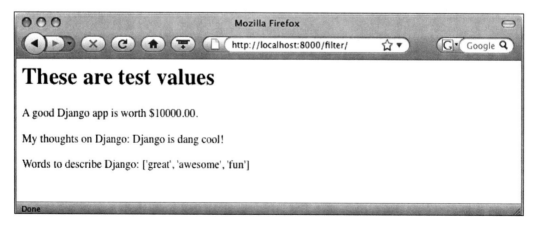

Notice that the first line now reads: **A good Django app is worth $10000.00.** with a proper U.S. currency formatting.

This worked great, but we are leaving ourselves open to a problem. If there is no value for the context variable price, or if it's not a numeric value, we'll get an error. By convention in Django, template filters should not raise any exceptions or throw errors. If something goes wrong, the filter should silently fail.

Let's put a block around the guts of the `uscurrency` function to trap any errors that could happen if the value of `c` isn't numeric.

In the `customtags/filtertest/templatetags/filtertest_extras.py` file, edit the highlighted code:

```python
from django import template

register = template.Library()

def uscurrency(c):
    try:
        if c > 0:
            return '$%.2f' % c
        else:
            return '-$%.2f' % (-1*c)
    except TypeError:
        return c
register.filter(uscurrency)
```

Now, if a value is passed that can't be formatted, the filter will return back the original value that was passed to it. Depending on your situation, you might want to return `None` or an empty string. That's up to you.

Replace profanities filter

This filter will take a list of swear words called PROFANITIES_LIST and make sure they are not present in a string. If they are found, the word will be replaced with the text *PROFANITY DELETED*.

> Django maintains a list of offensive English words called PROFANITIES_ LIST in the file `django/conf/global_settings.py`. Since we don't want to print the actual profanities here, we're going to use our own list with words such as "dang"and "darn". Outside of this example, you can just use the list by importing `settings.PROFANITIES_LIST`.

In the `customtags/filtertest/templatetags/filtertest_extras.py` file, add this code block to the bottom:

```python
def replace_profanities(value):
    PROFANITIES_LIST = ['dang', 'darn']
    replacement = '*PROFANITY REMOVED*'
    import re
    for word in PROFANITIES_LIST:
        regex = re.compile(r"\b%s\b" % word, re.I)
        if regex.search(value):
            value = regex.sub(replacement, value)
    return value
register.filter(replace_profanities)
```

In the `customtags/templates/filter_test.html` file, add the `replace_profanities` filter to the `thoughts` variable:

```html
<p>
My thoughts on Django:
{{ mythoughts|replace_profanities }}
</p>
```

Point your browser to the URL `http://localhost:8000/filter/` and you should see this:

In the `replace_profanities` function, we iterated through the `PROFANITIES_LIST` and did a regular expression search for each word. The word "dang" matched and was replaced with ***PROFANITY REMOVED***.

If you're not familiar with the regular expressions, one very important thing to notice in the function is this line:

```python
regex = re.compile(r"\b%s\b" % word, re.I)
```

The \b around the word makes sure that the regular expression uses word boundaries. This in turn makes sure that only the word by itself is matched, not substrings. For example, "Django is darn cool" would match for the word "darn", but "Django is darned cool" would not match because the word "darn" is inside the word "darned".

This kind of filtering can negatively affect performance on large lists of words or long strings of text (regular expressions being notoriously slow). If you're going to use this in an application with high traffic, you will probably want to use some sort of caching on your pages so that every request doesn't incur the processing overhead each time it loads. We'll talk about caching in a later chapter.

Filters that expect strings

If you are writing a filter that expects a string, you will probably want to make sure the value you are passed is a string and not an integer, list, and so on. If you try to run a string function such as upper() or lower() on a variable that is not a string, Python will throw an exception.

Instead of having to manually check or cast the value as a string, Django offers a function that will do it for us. You don't have to use it in your custom libraries, but it simplifies the handling of strings in filters that expect them.

In the customtags/filtertest/templatetags/filtertest_extras.py file, add the highlighted lines:

```
from django import template
from django.template.defaultfilters import stringfilter

register = template.Library()

def uscurrency(c):
    try:
        if c > 0:
            return '$%.2f' % c
        else:
            return '-$%.2f' % (-1*c)
    except TypeError:
        return c
register.filter('uscurrency', uscurrency)

def replace_profanities(value):
    PROFANITIES_LIST = ['dang', 'darn']
```

```
        replacement = '*PROFANITY REMOVED*'
        import re
        for word in PROFANITIES_LIST:
            regex = re.compile(r"\b%s\b" % word, re.I)
            if regex.search(value):
                value = regex.sub(replacement, value)
        return value
    replace_profanities = stringfilter(replace_profanities)
    register.filter(replace_profanities)
```

With the addition of `stringfilter`, the argument `value` is automatically converted to a string before the function processes. This will catch any problems if the filter is attached to a list, integer, and so on.

 `stringfilter` can also be called using decorator notation if you are using Python 2.4 or higher. See the online documentation for the syntax.

In-list filter

Let's make a filter that tests if a string is present in a list. We'll make it return a Boolean `True` or `False` if the string is in the list, and we can use it in conjunction with an `{% if %}` tag. (It's also a good example of a template filter that takes an argument.)

In the `customtags/filtertest/templatetags/filtertest_extras.py` file, add this code block to the end:

```
def in_list(value, arg):
    if type(value) != list:
        return False
    elif arg in value:
        return True
    else:
        return False
register.filter(in_list)
```

In the `customtags/templates/filter_test.html` file, edit the highlighted block:

```
{% load filtertest_extras %}
<h1>These are test values</h1>
<p>A good Django app is worth {{ myprice|uscurrency }}.</p>
<p>
My thoughts on Django: {{ mythoughts|replace_profanities }}
</p>

{% if mywords|in_list:"great" %}
```

```
<p>They think Django is great!</p>
{% else %}
<p>They don't think Django is great.</p>
{% endif %}
```

Point your browser to the URL `http://localhost:8000/filter/` and you should see this:

For this filter, we did things a little differently. We returned a Boolean `True` or `False` as the argument to the `{% if %}` tag. This is a great way to do conditional logic on a value in those cases where the tags `if`, `ifequal`, and `ifnotequal` don't provide the functionality you need.

Writing your own template tags

Template tags require more steps to build because they are more flexible and can do more complex tasks than filters. Some of the biggest differences between tags and filters are that tags don't have to be attached to any values and they can take multiple arguments.

Writing a tag is a two-step process. First, you compile the tag text into a *Node*, which is a "chunk" of template that can be rendered. Second, you render the *Node* into output and return it to the template.

Creating another sample application

Let's leave the `filtertest` application alone and create a new application called `tagtest` to use as our sandbox for testing custom template tags.

In the `/projects/customttags` directory, run the `startapp` command:

```
$ python manage.py startapp tagtest
```

In `customtags/settings.py`, add our new `tagtest` application to the `INSTALLED_APPS` tuple. Add the highlighted line:

```
INSTALLED_APPS = (
    'customtags.filtertest',
    'customtags.tagtest',
)
```

In `customtags/urls.py`, add the highlighted line:

```
from django.conf.urls.defaults import *

urlpatterns = patterns('',
    (r'^filter/', 'customtags.filtertest.views.test'),
    (r'^tag/', 'customtags.tagtest.views.test'),
)
```

Create a new file called `tag_test.html` in the `customtags/templates` directory and add the following line. (This is just the start. We'll add more to this as we create some tags.)

```
<h1>These are test tags</h1>
```

As in the case of the `filtertest` application we wrote earlier, we won't create any models for the `tagtest` application. Instead, we'll pass variables in the view to our template context.

Finally, in the `customtags/tagtest/views.py` file, add these lines:

```
from django.http import HttpResponse
from django.template import Context, loader
import datetime

def test(request):
    t = loader.get_template('tag_test.html')
    c = Context({
        'current_time': datetime.datetime.now(),
    })
    return HttpResponse(t.render(c))
```

Point your browser to the URL `http://localhost:8000/tag/` and you should see this:

Adding the template library

Just as we did with the `filtertest` application, we need to create a folder underneath our application called `templatetags` to hold our library files.

Create a directory at `customtags/tagtest/templatetags` and a file underneath called `tagtest_extras.py` with the following lines:

```
from django import template

register = template.Library()
```

Create a blank file called `__init__.py` in the `templatetags` directory.

Template tag syntax

In its simplest form, calling a tag in a template looks like this:

```
{% tagname %}
```

The tag `tagname` will be called and any output from the tag will be put in its place in the template. (Tags don't have to output anything.) If you want to pass arguments to tags, you can do so by separating them with spaces:

```
{% tagname argument1 argument2 argument3 %}
```

Arguments can be template context variables, strings, integers, and so on, but all arguments to tags will be considered strings. If you are passing an integer argument, for example, you'll have to convert it to an integer before you can use it numerically.

A simple tag example

Before we can break down the steps of parsing a tag, we'll need to create a very simple example to work with. Let's create a tag that prints out a pleasant greeting.

In the `customtags/tagtest/templatetags/tagtest_extras.py` file, add the highlighted lines:

```python
from django import template

register = template.Library()

def do_say_greeting(parser, token):
    return SayGreetingNode()
register.tag('say_greeting', do_say_greeting)

class SayGreetingNode(template.Node):
    def render(self, context):
        return "Hello, it's nice to meet you."
```

In the `customtags/templates/tag_test.html` file, add the highlighted lines:

```html
{% load tagtest_extras %}

<h1>These are test tags</h1>

{% say_greeting %}
```

Point your browser to the URL `http://localhost:8000/tag/` and you should see this:

Writing a tag is more involved than writing a filter, so let's break down what's happening in this example.

The compilation function

As we saw, parsing template tags is a two-step process. The first step is the compilation function that splits the arguments and performs any necessary logic to make sure the tag was called properly.

In our example, we don't have any arguments and so the compilation function has very little do to. It simply returns a subclass of `Node` called `SayGreetingNode` that we defined. Notice that the function is prefixed with `do_`, which is a Django convention for naming compilation functions.

The compilation function takes two arguments: `parser`, the template parser object that is automatically passed to it, and `token`, which holds all the information necessary to parse the tag. The string `token.contents` is a string containing everything from the tag between the `{%` and `%}` characters.

In this example, `token.contents` only contains the name of the tag being called, so we don't need to do anything with it. In a later example, we'll practice splitting `token.contents` into the tag name and any arguments passed.

The template node subclass

The second step of rendering a custom template is to define a subclass that the compilation function can call. This subclass of `Template.Node` must have a `render()` method that the template engine will call.

In our simple greeting example, the subclass is `SayGreetingNode`. It contains the required `render()` method that returns a string with our greeting.

Registering our custom tag

Just as we did with our custom filters, we need to register the tag with the template system. We do this by calling `register.tag()` directly underneath our compilation function:

```
def do_say_greeting(parser, token):
    return SayGreetingNode()
register.tag('say_greeting', do_say_greeting)
```

The first argument to `register.tag` is the name of the custom tag as we will call it in our template. The second argument is the name of the compilation function.

This example was very simple, but serves as a good demonstration of what is required to create a custom template tag. Let's create another example that takes the concept one step further by passing an argument.

All work and no play tag

This tag will output the text "*All work and no play makes Jack a dull boy.*" as many times as the user wants, as dictated by a numeric argument to the tag.

Before we create the code, edit the file `customtags/templates/tag_test.html` to look like this:

```
{% load tagtest_extras %}

<h1>These are test tags</h1>

{% all_work_no_play 10 %}
```

The `all_work_no_play` tag has not been created yet, but notice that we are passing the number `10` as an argument.

In the file `customtags/tagtest/templatetags/tagtest_extras.py`, add this code to the end of the file:

```
class AllWorkNode(template.Node):
    def __init__(self, repetitions):
        self.repetitions = repetitions
    def render(self, context):
        msg = "All work and no play makes Jack a dull boy. "
        return self.repetitions * msg

def do_all_work(parser, token):
    tag_name, repetitions = token.split_contents()
    repetitions = int(repetitions)
    return AllWorkNode(repetitions)
register.tag('all_work_no_play', do_all_work)
```

This tag has a few more lines than our greeting example. We'll start with the `do_all_work` function. The first line splits `token.contents` (the raw string of the tag between the `{% %}` delimiters) into the tag name and the argument:

```
tag_name, repetitions = token.split_contents()
```

The first piece returned from splitting the `token.contents` string will always be the name of the tag.

As we saw earlier, one very important item to note about the arguments and tags is that they will only come in as strings, regardless of what they were in the template. In this case, the number `10` is returned as a string, not an integer. The next line casts the value properly:

```
repetitions = int(repetitions)
```

Now that we have parsed out the arguments, we have the information we need to call our template node subclass. But wait! There is a potential danger lurking in our example. What if the template author forgets to put an argument in the tag? When we call token.split_contents(), we are expecting two values back and so this would cause an error.

To ensure that the user specifies an argument with the tag, we have to add some additional code to trap the error. Add the highlighted lines:

```
def do_all_work(parser, token):
    tag_name = token.contents.split()[0]
    try:
        tag_name, repetitions = token.split_contents()
        repetitions = int(repetitions)
    except ValueError:
        raise template.TemplateSyntaxError, \
            "%r tag missing integer argument" \
            % tag_name
    return AllWorkNode(repetitions)
register.tag('all_work_no_play', do_all_work)
```

If the template author forgets to specify the integer argument, a template error will be raised.

The last line registers the tag and gives it the name all_work_no_play that we call it with in the template:

```
register.tag('all_work_no_play', do_all_work)
```

Besides the render() function that we saw in the previous example, the AllWorkNode class also defines its constructor. The constructor takes the repetitive argument that is assigned to an instance variable self.repetitions.

If you aren't familiar with objects, just understand that Python will automatically call a special method called __init__() (if it exists) when a class is instantiated. This special function is called the **constructor**. We have to assign the argument passed to the constructor to an **instance variable**, which is a variable assigned to our object that other class methods can use.

In this example, assigning the value of the argument repetitions to self.repetitions means that the render() method of our class will be able to use it.

With everything in place, point your browser to the URL http://localhost:8000/ tag/ and you should see this:

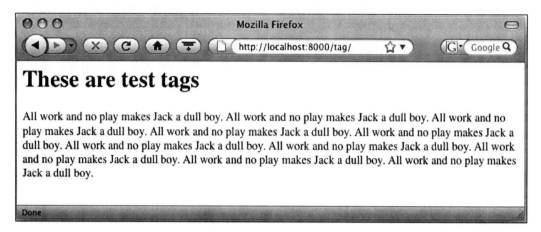

Try changing the argument to the tag to 100 and refresh the page. You should see ten times as many sentences.

Passing a template variable to a tag

For our final tag, we'll kill two birds with one stone. Let's build a tag that can take a context variable as an argument and set a new context variable that we can use later in the same template. Let's pass the current date to a tag and have it return tomorrow's date.

Let's set up the example. Edit the file customtags/templates/tag_test.html to look like this:

```
{% load tagtest_extras %}

<h1>These are test tags</h1>

Tomorrow is {% tomorrow current_time %}
```

Notice that we are calling a tag called tomorrow with the argument current_time. (Remember that we specified current_time in the view when we set up this example earlier.)

Add this block to the file `customtags/tagtest/templatetags/tagtest_extras.py` at the end of the file:

```
class TomorrowNode(template.Node):
    def __init__(self, current_date):
        self.current_date = template.Variable(current_date)
    def render(self, context):
        try:
            current_date = self.current_date.resolve(context)
            import datetime
            tomorrow = current_date + \
                datetime.timedelta(days=1)
            return tomorrow
        except template.VariableDoesNotExist:
            return ''

def do_tomorrow(parser, token):
    tag_name = token.contents.split()[0]
    try:
        tag_name, current_time = token.split_contents()
    except ValueError:
        raise template.TemplateSyntaxError, \
            "%r tag requires a datetime argument" \
            % tag_name
    return TomorrowNode(current_time)
register.tag('tomorrow', do_tomorrow)
```

This code is very similar to what we saw in the previous example. We are splitting the token to get the tag name and arguments, making sure the argument was passed, and returning a node.

Using a context variable such as `current_time` as an argument provides an extra challenge. Remember that arguments are parsed into the compilation function as strings. In our example, when we parse out the `token.contents` string, we will be left with two strings: `tomorrow` and `current_date`. In order to turn the string `current_date` into the value of the context variable, we have to write some additional code.

Looking at the class `TomorrowNode`, we have `__init__` (the constructor) and our `render` method. In the constructor, look at the syntax used to assign the `current_date` argument:

```
self.current_date = template.Variable(current_date)
```

We are telling Django that `current_date` is a string that represents a template context variable. We can't actually resolve that variable into a value. That happens next in the render step:

```
current_date = self.current_date.resolve(context)
```

We have the current template context available to us in the `render` function so that we can finally figure out what the value of `current_date` is! From this point, we use `datetime.timedelta` to figure out what `current_date` plus one day is.

Point your browser to the URL `http://localhost:8000/tag/` and you should see this:

(Your date will be different because your current time will be different.)

Modifying the context through a tag

Finally, let's do an extra-cool thing. Django's template system doesn't let you set values from within templates, but template tags can. (Remember from the beginning of the chapter when we said template tags can do anything?)

Let's change the `TomorrowNode` class slightly to set a new context variable instead of returning a string. In `tagtest_extras.py`, change the highlighted lines:

```
class TomorrowNode(template.Node):
    def __init__(self, current_date):
        self.current_date = template.Variable(current_date)

    def render(self, context):
        try:
            import datetime
            current_date = self.current_date.resolve(context)
            tomorrow = current_date + \
                datetime.timedelta(days=1)
```

```
            context['tomorrow_time'] = tomorrow
            return ''
        except template.VariableDoesNotExist:
            return ''
```

In the earlier chapter about the template context, we saw that context acts like a dictionary, and adding new values is done with the traditional Python dictionary syntax. In this case, we're adding a new context variable by specifying it as the key `tomorrow_time` and assigning it the value of our `tomorrow` variable.

We're returning an empty string. If we didn't, the value `None` would be written out in the template.

Edit the `customtags/templates/tag_test.html` file to look like this:

```
{% load tagtest_extras %}

<h1>These are test tags</h1>

{% tomorrow current_time %}

<p>Today is {{ current_time }}</p>
<p>Tomorrow is {{ tomorrow_time }}</p>
```

The `tomorrow` tag is called, but doesn't return any values. Instead, it sets the template context variable `tomorrow_time` that we can then use a couple of lines later.

Point your browser to the URL `http://localhost:8000/tag/` and you should see this:

Summary

In this chapter, we learned how to write our own custom tags and filters to extend the default functionality of the Django template system. We looked at the structure of the built-in tags and filters as a starting point for creating our own.

We explored how template filters are constructed and registered by the template system. We also saw how they are loaded and called in the template, and how to pass an argument to a filter.

We wrote our own filters to format U.S. currency values, remove profanities from text, and see if a value was present in a list.

We looked at the structure of template tags, seeing how they have a two-step process of compiling and returning a node. We learned how arguments are passed to templates and how to parse them into their values. We also saw how to pass template variables as arguments to tags and to add new context variables inside a tag.

This chapter was much more involved than others we have worked with. Be proud of getting through these more advanced topics and go forth with confidence that you'll be able to extend the template system if you get in a jam!

In the next chapter, we will learn about the concept of Pagination.

8
Pagination

An important aspect of web usability is to break the data returned by your application into manageable pages. Presenting hundreds of records on a single page can result in pages that are large in size and result sets that are hard to scan for information. Django provides a `Paginator` library that makes it easy to split your results into smaller sets.

In this chapter we will:

- Create a test application for experimenting with pagination
- Learn how to implement the Paginator using the interactive Django shell
- See the SQL executed when using the Paginator
- Construct a view using pagination
- Implement navigational links for pagination in the template
- Use pagination with generic views

An Overview

Without the paginator library, we would have to write a lot of code by hand to break our data into pages: SQL offsets, limits, calculating the number of pages, and so on. Django's paginator library does all of this grunt work for us and wraps it all into a nice object that we can pass to the template context.

Implementing the paginator library is simple and requires only a few steps:

1. Retrieve our `queryset` in the view using the database API
2. Pass that `queryset` object to the `paginator` object
3. Retrieve a current page object from the paginator object
4. Pass the current page object to our template via the context

A `querystring` variable maintains the state of what page we are on in the queryset so that we can navigate back and forth through the pages. The paginator takes care of handling invalid page numbers, serving 404 pages, and so on.

Verifying our application setup

We will use our ongoing press application to experiment with the pagination library. Before we start, let's make sure that the application is set up properly, in case you've been skipping around chapters. If you've been following along, then you can skim through the next few sections that make sure your application is set up properly. But pay close attention to the URL listings to make sure that yours match the ones we're using.

Verifying the application

You should have an application called `press` located at `/projects/mycompany/press`. If you don't, run this command in the `/projects/mycompany` directory:

```
$ python manage.py startapp press
```

You should now have a `/projects/mycompany/press` directory.

Verifying the configuration

Make sure that the application is listed in your `mycompany/settings.py` file in the `INSTALLED_APPS` tuple:

```
INSTALLED_APPS = (
    'django.contrib.auth',
    'django.contrib.contenttypes',
    'django.contrib.sessions',
    'django.contrib.sites',
    'django.contrib.admin',
    'mycompany.press',
)
```

 If your `INSTALLED_APPS` setting looks different, that's OK as long as `mycompany.press` is listed.

Verifying the URL configuration

In your `mycompany/urls.py` file, you should have the highlighted URL pattern:

```
urlpatterns = patterns('',
    (r'^admin/(.*)', admin.site.root),
    (r'^press/', include('mycompany.press.urls')),
)
```

In your `mycompany/press/urls.py` file, make sure the highlighted configuration exists and points to the `press_list` view. (In an earlier chapter, we used a generic view.)

```
urlpatterns = patterns('',
    (r'detail/(?P<pid>\d+)/$','mycompany.press.views.detail'),
    (r'list/$','mycompany.press.views.press_list'),
    (r'latest/$','mycompany.press.views.latest'),
    (r'$','django.views.generic.simple.redirect_to',
        {'url': '/press/list/'})
)
```

Verifying the model

In the `mycompany/press/models.py` file, make sure you have this `PressRelease` model:

```
class PressRelease(models.Model):
    title = models.CharField(max_length=100)
    body = models.TextField()
    pub_date = models.DateTimeField()
    author = models.CharField(max_length=100)

    class Meta:
        get_latest_by = 'pub_date'

    def get_absolute_url(self):
        return '/press/detail/%d/' % self.id

    def __unicode__(self):
        return self.title
```

If you didn't already have the model listed, run the `syncdb` command to add the new tables. (You can run it again to make sure, it won't hurt anything.)

```
$ python manage.py syncdb
```

Verifying the view

We will be working with the `press_list` view shortly to add pagination, but this is what we will be starting with. In the `mycompany/press/views.py` file, make sure you have a `press_list` view:

```
def press_list(request):
    '''
    Returns a list of press releases
    '''
    pl = get_list_or_404(PressRelease)
    t = loader.get_template('press/list.html')
    c = Context({'press_list': pl})
    return HttpResponse(t.render(c))
```

While you are working in the `mycompany/press/views.py` file, make sure you have the necessary import statements at the top:

```
from django.http import HttpResponse
from django.templates import Context, loader
from press.models import PressRelease
```

Adding test records

To effectively test pagination, we need to have enough records in the database to be able to break them into pages. We could do this manually in the admin application, but it would be tedious. Instead, let's use the Django interactive shell to programmatically add some test records.

Run the `shell` command to start the interactive shell:

```
$ python manage.py shell
```

You should see something like the following; the three brackets indicate that you are ready to start entering Python and Django commands:

```
Python 2.5.1 (r251:54869, Apr 18 2007, 22:08:04)
[GCC 4.0.1 (Apple Computer, Inc. build 5367)] on darwin
Type "help", "copyright", "credits" or "license" for more information.
(InteractiveConsole)
>>>
```

Enter the following commands (without the three brackets) to get rid of any press release records you might have saved:

```
>>> from mycompany.press.models import PressRelease
>>> for p in PressRelease.objects.all():
>>>     p.delete()
```

Now we'll import the datetime module, and run a looping code block to create and save 52 records:

```
>>> import datetime
>>> for x in range(52):
...     p = PressRelease.objects.create(
...         title='This is a press release %d' % x,
...         body='This is the body',
...         pub_date=datetime.datetime.now(),
...         author='John Doe',
...     )
...     p.save()
>>>
```

Now we have 52 records that we'll be able to retrieve to test the pagination.

Exploring pagination using the Django shell

Before we create any views to paginate our results, we can test most of the concepts in the Django shell. This will make it easier to see the various methods and properties instead of switching between views and templates.

First, let's import the model and retrieve a queryset:

```
>>> from mycompany.press.models import PressRelease
>>> pl = PressRelease.objects.all()
>>> len(pl)
52
```

We can import the Paginator class, and pass it our queryset object and an argument of 10 records per page:

```
>>> from django.core.paginator import Paginator
>>> p = Paginator(pl, 10)
```

Let's look at some of the properties of our `Paginator` object. (The code comments are provided for explanation; you don't have to type them.)

```
>>> # per_page gives us the number of records per page
>>> p.per_page
10
>>>
>>> # num_pages gives us the number of pages of records
>>> p.num_pages
6
>>>
>>> # count gives us the number of total records
>>> p.count
52
>>>
>>> # page_range gives us a list of page numbers
>>> p.page_range
[1, 2, 3, 4, 5, 6]
```

These properties are useful, but we need to call the `Paginator.page()` method with a page number argument to construct our page of records:

```
>>> # pass a page number to the page method
>>> cp = p.page(1)
>>>
>>> # number gives us number of the current page
>>> cp.number
1
>>>
>>> # has_previous returns True if there is a page
>>> # before the current page
>>> cp.has_previous()
False
>>>
>>> # has_next returns True if there is a page
>>> # after the current page
>>> cp.has_next()
True
>>>
>>> # has_other_pages returns True if there are pages
>>> # other than the current page
>>> cp.has_other_pages()
True
>>>
>>> # start_index tells us the position in the overall
```

```
>>> # queryset for the first record on the current page
>>> cp.start_index()
1
>>>
>>> # end_index tells us the position in the overall
>>> # queryset for the last record on the current page
>>> cp.end_index()
10
>>>
>>> # next_page_number tells us the page number after
>>> # the current page
>>> cp.next_page_number()
2
>>>
>>> # previous_page_number tells us the page number
>>> # before the current page
>>> cp.previous_page_number()
0
>>>
>>> # object_list shows us the objects in the current page
>>> cp.object_list
[<PressRelease: This is a press release 0>, <PressRelease: This
is a press release 1>, <PressRelease: This is a press release 2>,
<PressRelease: This is a press release 3>, <PressRelease: This is
a press release 4>, <PressRelease: This is a press release 5>,
<PressRelease: This is a press release 6>, <PressRelease: This is
a press release 7>, <PressRelease: This is a press release 8>,
<PressRelease: This is a press release 9>]
```

Using these methods and properties, we have everything we need to build our view and templates. We'll use them in our view to retrieve the objects, loop through them, and build the navigation to go forward and back through the pages.

Examining database performance

At a first glance, it appears that the way Django paginates will retrieve all the records and then just "slice off" whatever the current page uses. Luckily, this is not the case. Django selects full records only when they are iterated over (also known as "lazy evaluation"). If it didn't, large record sets could kill the performance because it would retrieve all the columns for all the records just to use a page of them.

In the Django shell, we can look at a variable called connection.queries to watch a running list of SQL queries that have been executed. You'll see in the example that follows that Django only retrieves the records for the current page, and only does so after we loop through them.

If you have the interactive shell open, stop it by typing the `exit` function and restart it so that we clear out anything in memory before trying the next example:

```
>>> exit()
$ python manage.py shell
```

With the interactive shell open, try this example:

```
>>> from django.db import connection
>>> from mycompany.press.models import PressRelease
>>> from django.core.paginator import Paginator
>>>
>>> pl = PressRelease.objects.all()
>>>
>>> # No queries have been run yet
>>> connection.queries
[]
>>> p = Paginator(pl, 2)
>>>
>>> # Still no queries, even though we called the paginator
>>> connection.queries
[]
>>> cur_page = p.page(1)
>>>
>>> # Calling the page resulted in our first query but all
>>> # it did was select a count, not the records
>>> connection.queries
[{'time': '0.002', 'sql': 'SELECT COUNT(*) FROM "press_
pressrelease"'}]
>>>
>>> for item in cur_page.object_list:
...     print item.title
...
This is a press release 0
This is a press release 1
>>>
>>> # Now we have two total queries - notice the limit clause
>>> # used in the query that only calls 2 rows
>>> connection.queries
[{'time': '0.003', 'sql': 'SELECT COUNT(*) FROM "press_
pressrelease"'}, {'time': '0.001', 'sql': 'SELECT "press_
pressrelease"."id", "press_pressrelease"."title", "press_
pressrelease"."body", "press_pressrelease"."pub_date", "press_
pressrelease"."author" FROM "press_pressrelease" LIMIT 2'}]
>>>
```

connection.queries will only be used when debugging is enabled in your settings.py file.

As you can see, Django only selected the columns from the rows when we looped through the object list. Also, it was careful to use a limit clause when the SQL was executed so that only two rows were retrieved.

Allowing for empty result sets

By default, the Paginator class allows you to pass empty object lists. If you'd prefer to automatically return a 404 page if there are no records, you can override the allow_empty_first_page parameter:

```
p = Paginator(pl, 2, allow_empty_first_page=False)
```

 Warning: Don't try to use the get_object_or_404 shortcut when getting your result set. get_object_or_404 returns a list, not a queryset. Use the allow_empty_first_page argument if you want a 404 page when there are no records.

Preventing orphaned records

In the example result set that we have been using, we have 52 records. If we are allowing 10 records per page, we will end up with six pages, the last one having only two records (for example, 1-10, 11-20, 21-30, 31-40, 41-50, 51-52).

Paginator allows us to stick these two end records to the last results page to prevent the page with just a couple of records. These records are considered "orphans" and by specifying the number of orphans, we end up with only five pages of results, the last page having 12 items instead of 10:

```
>>> from django.core.paginator import Paginator
>>> from mycompany.press.models import PressRelease
>>> pl = PressRelease.objects.all()
>>> len(pl)
52
>>> p = Paginator(pl, 10, orphans=2)
>>> p.num_pages
5
>>> p.page_range
[1, 2, 3, 4, 5]
>>>
```

```
>>> # This page will have 10 objects
>>> p4 = p.page(4)
>>> len(p4.object_list)
10
>>>
>>> # The last page has 12 objects because the
>>> # orphans are added automatically
>>> p5 = p.page(5)
>>> len(p5.object_list)
12
```

Using pagination in your views

Now that we've used the Django shell to interactively look at the methods and
properties of the `Paginator` and `Page` objects, let's use that knowledge in an
actual view.

Creating the view

In the `mycompany/press/views.py` file, edit the `press_list` view function to look
like this and add the import statement to load the pagination module:

```
from django.core.paginator import Paginator

def press_list(request):
    '''
    Returns a list of press releases
    '''

    pl = PressRelease.objects.all()
    p = Paginator(pl, 10)
    cur_page = p.page(request.GET.get('page', 1))

    t = loader.get_template('press/list.html')
    c = Context({
        'press_list': cur_page.object_list,
        'page_obj': cur_page,
    })
    return HttpResponse(t.render(c))
```

We're using the `Paginator` the same way we did in the examples from the Django
shell. We pass two items into the template context: `press_list` and `page_obj`.
`press_list`. While `press_list` is a list of objects from the current page, `page_obj` is
an object representing the current page of results. These two items are all we need to
be able to return the records and navigation on the page.

Retrieving the current position from the URL

The line from the view that gets the page number from a URL parameter deserves a closer look and explanation:

```
cur_page = p.page(request.GET.get('page', 1))
```

A good rule of thumb when building web applications is to never trust data that comes from GET or POST, and this is not an exception. We're getting a variable called page from the URL, and if it's not present, we are using the integer 1.

We aren't casting page as an integer (querystring parameters are evaluated as Unicode strings, even if they represent numbers) or even making sure it's a number. Why? The Paginator class does this for us. If an invalid page number is passed, either a number outside the range of pages or an invalid value such as a non-digit, the Paginator will automatically return a 404 page.

 Remember: Page objects are 1-based, so the first page will be 1, not 0.

Putting navigation into the templates

Before we can see the output of our work in a browser, we need to put together the template and build in the appropriate navigation to go to the next and previous pages.

Edit the mycompany/templates/press/list.html file to look like this:

```html
<html>
<head>
<title>Press Releases</title>
</head>
<body>
<h1>Press Releases</h1>
<ul>
{% for press in press_list %}
<li>
<a href="{{ press.get_absolute_url }}">
{{ press.title }}</a>
</li>
{% endfor %}
</ul>
<p>
Page {{ page_obj.number }} of {{ page_obj.paginator.num_pages }}
```

```
</p>
<p>
{% if page_obj.has_previous %}
<a href="?page={{ page_obj.previous_page_number }}">Previous</a>
{% else %}
Previous
{% endif %}
 | 
{% if page_obj.has_next %}
<a href="?page={{ page_obj.next_page_number }}">Next</a>
{% else %}
Next
{% endif %}
</p>
</body>
</html>
```

 If you have been following along with the previous chapters, you'll notice that we're not using template inheritance with this example. This is intentional to keep the example simple. Feel free to go back and add it afterwards for good practice.

In the first part of our template, we are iterating over the objects from the current page:

```
<ul>
{% for press in press_list %}
<li>
<a href="{{ press.get_absolute_url }}">
{{ press.title }}</a>
</li>
{% endfor %}
</ul>
```

In the second part of the template, we are using the properties of the `page` object `page_obj` to write out the navigation between the pages:

```
{% if page_obj.has_previous %}
<a href="?page={{ page_obj.previous_page_number }}">Previous</a>
{% else %}
Previous
{% endif %}
 | 
{% if page_obj.has_next %}
```

```
<a href="?page={{ page_obj.next_page_number }}">Next</a>
{% else %}
Next
{% endif %}
```

Using the Boolean values for `has_previous` and `has_next`, we determine if the words "Previous" and "Next" should be hyperlinked or just static text.

Point your browser to the URL `http://localhost:8000/press/list/` and you should see this:

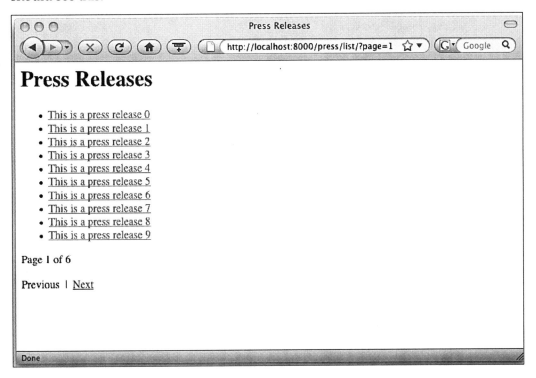

Pagination with generic views

As we discussed in Chapter 2, generic views are used to cut down on the number of boilerplate views we end up writing in many web applications. The paginating results in these pages are also very common, and are built into the handling of generic views.

Setting up our generic list view

Instead of replacing our current list view, let's add another URL configuration to the mycompany/press/urls.py file. Add the highlighted lines:

```
from django.conf.urls.defaults import *
from mycompany.press.models import PressRelease

press_list_dict = {
    'queryset': PressRelease.objects.all(),
    'template_name': 'press/list.html',
    'allow_empty': False,
    'template_object_name': 'press',
    'paginate_by': 10,
}

urlpatterns = patterns('',
    (r'detail/(?P<pid>\d+)/$','mycompany.press.views.detail'),
    (r'list/$','mycompany.press.views.press_list'),
    (r'list2/',
        'django.views.generic.list_detail.object_list',
        press_list_dict),
    (r'latest/$','mycompany.press.views.latest'),
    (r'$','django.views.generic.simple.redirect_to',
        {'url': '/press/list/'})
)
```

 If you have been following along with earlier chapters, the highlighted import statement press_list_dict dictionary will already be in your file. Edit your code to look like the current example.

This is similar to what we did in our chapter about the generic views. In our press_list_dict dictionary, we've added an additional key called paginate_by.

 The second URL configuration does not have a dollar sign at the end of the first element in the tuple. This is important because it allows the URL to match with or without the ?page=*n* parameter.

As of the time of this writing, you cannot specify the allow_empty_first_page and orphan parameters to generic views.

Point your browser to the URL http://localhost:8000/press/list2/ and you should see the same output as before. (This URL uses generic views)

Generically calling the last page

One cool feature in generic view pagination is the ability to use the string `last` in the URL instead of a number.

For example, instead of this URL:

```
http://localhost:8000/press/list2/?page=6
```

You can use this:

```
http://localhost:8000/press/list2/?page=last
```

With this trick, you can create a link somewhere in your site to the last page of press releases without having to know how many pages of results exist. Often the last page of results has the most recent items, so you can use this to display only the latest.

Summary

In this chapter, we learned how to break our result sets into smaller pieces with the pagination library. We configured our press application and populated it with enough records to test out the concepts using the interactive Django shell. We looked at the properties of the `Paginator` and `Page` objects, and what their values represent.

We put these concepts into practice in a view, and built a template with the appropriate navigation to view the pages that made up our results set. Finally, we explored how to use pagination when using generic views.

In the next chapter, we will learn how to customize the look and feel of the automatic admin application.

9
Customizing the Admin Look and Feel

The automatic admin application (aka "the admin") is an amazing feature of Django that saves countless hours of routine development work. To add that extra "finishing touch" to your application, you may want to change the color scheme of the admin pages to match your site, change some of the default page headers, and add outside links to the admin dashboard.

In this chapter, we will:

- Explore how admin templates are structured
- Override the necessary templates to customize the appearance of the admin
- Change the default header of the admin pages
- Add navigation links to the top of the admin page
- Add an additional box of links to the admin dashboard
- Override the admin stylesheet to match your site's color scheme

 We're will not talk about how to change the functionality of the admin, since that's thoroughly documented in Django's online documentation. We're going to look at how to make the admin appear with the same look and feel as the rest of your site.

Overriding the admin templates

Before we can start modifying the admin templates, we need to explore their structure. The templates used for the admin are no different than other Django templates, and you already know everything needed to work with them. We don't want to edit the existing admin templates as they are part of the Django source code. If we edit them, we might lose our changes when updating Django as they could get overridden with the new files. Instead, we will override the files and leave the originals untouched.

Leveraging the template loader

In an earlier chapter, we talked about the `app_directories` template loader that looks for a directory called `templates` underneath your individual applications. This is how the admin templates "automatically" appear. They are found in a directory in the Django admin source code. (We'll look at them shortly.)

In our `mycompany/settings.py` file, we use both the `filesystem` and `app_directories` loaders:

```
TEMPLATE_LOADERS = (
    'django.template.loaders.filesystem.load_template_source',
    'django.template.loaders.app_directories.load_template_source',
)
```

The order of the loaders is important. Using the `filesystem` loader first allows us to create an `admin` directory under our site's templates folder that will be used to override the admin templates.

Our template files are located in this directory, as defined in the `TEMPLATE_DIRS` value in the `mycompany/settings.py` file:

```
/projects/mycompany/templates/
```

In our `templates` directory, we will create a subdirectory called `admin` that holds our admin templates. Using this setup, the template loader will first look in the `/projects/mycompany/templates/admin` directory for a template file. If it doesn't find the file, Django will use the default admin file. This is perfect for us because we only need to create the files that we want to override.

Locating the admin template files

Let's look at the admin templates that ship with your Django distribution. You'll need to know where Django is installed on your machine, which varies depending on how you set it up.

If you download and install a release of Django, your files will likely be under your Python `site-packages` directory. To find where that directory is, launch the Python interactive shell and enter these commands:

```
>>> import distutils.sysconfig
>>> print distutils.sysconfig.get_python_lib()
/Library/Python/2.5/site-packages
```

From this example, you can see that the `site-packages` directory on my Macintosh is located in the `/Library/Python/2.5/` directory. Yours may be different. Once you locate the `site-packages` directory, browse it for a directory called `django`. This directory will contain the Django source code files.

Exploring the admin template files

In your Django source code directory, browse for the `contrib/admin/templates/` `admin` directory and you'll see about twenty-five HTML files. It may seem like a lot, but there are only a few that we'll be concerned with. The others are just includes or snippets that we won't need to customize.

Here are the main files and their purposes:

- `base.html`: This is the highest parent template. We will not do any customization in it, but there are some important extra blocks to look at.
- `base_site.html`: This file has the page title and header text. It extends `base.html` and we will do most of our customizations in it.
- `change_list.html`: This is the list of objects you can edit when you choose one of your apps on the home page.
- `change_form.html`: This is the form that's shown when editing an object.
- `index.html`: This is the home or "dashboard" page of the admin app that lists all the apps you can manipulate. (We'll be adding some extra links to this page.)

Inspecting the base.html template

We won't be editing or overriding the `base.html` file because Django has done much of the heavy lifting for us. On lines seven and eight of the file, there are blocks that allow us to add extra information into the `head` of the HTML document from within the child templates:

```
{% block extrastyle %}{% endblock %}
{% block extrahead %}{% endblock %}
```

When we start writing our own admin templates, we'll use these `extrastyle` and `extrahead` blocks to our advantage and inject extra CSS and JavaScript into the resulting HTML output.

Inspecting the base_site.html template

This simple file is the ideal place to do most of the customization work for our admin. For example, we can change the title and the text header at the top of all the admin pages by editing the `title` and `branding` blocks:

```
{% block title %}{{ title }} | {% trans 'Django site admin' %}
{% endblock %}

{% block branding %}
<h1 id="site-name">{% trans 'Django administration' %}</h1>
{% endblock %}

{% block nav-global %}{% endblock %}
```

The last empty block, `nav-global`, allows you to add content to the bottom of the colored header underneath the branding text.

Since we'll be editing the title and branding text for our site, we'll want to copy this `base_site.html` file to our `templates/admin` directory. We'll also be adding extra CSS information to this file to make the color scheme match that of ours.

 What are these `trans` tags? They are used by Django's internationalization (i18n) libraries to automatically translate the text into the user's language preference.

Inspecting the index.html template

This file controls the dashboard page you see when logging into the admin. All the applications you have permission to manipulate are listed in blocks such as **Auth**, **Flatpages**, **Press**, and **Sites** in the following example:

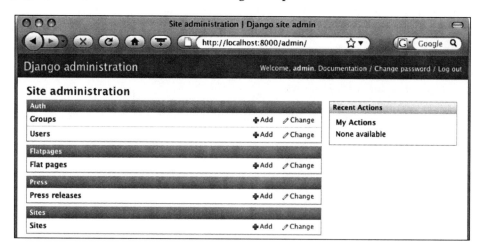

We can add additional content above or below these blocks by adding it to the appropriate place in the `index.html` file:

```
{% block content %}
<div id="content-main">

We can put HTML here to make it appear above the
boxes for the applications.

{% if app_list %}
    {% for app in app_list %}
```

By adding content in the highlighted area, we can add our own links and content to the main admin page.

Inspecting the change_list.html template

The change list is the main list of objects inside an application (such as the press release application) that we can edit. We won't be editing or overriding this file, but notice the alternating color scheme on the list. The template calls a custom tag that renders the `change_list_results.html` file:

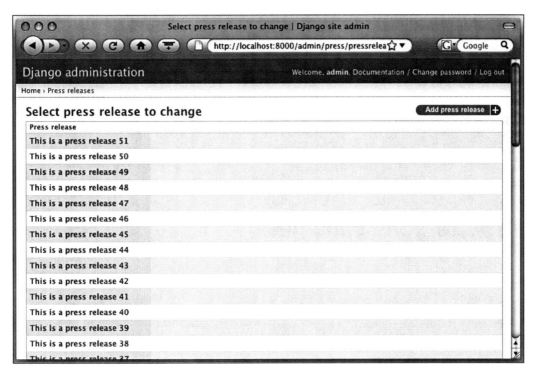

The colors are controlled by the `row1` and `row2` classes applied by the `cycle` tag in the `change_list_results.html` file:

```
<tbody>
{% for result in results %}
<tr class="{% cycle 'row1' 'row2' %}">{% for item in result %}
{{ item }}{% endfor %}</tr>
{% endfor %}
</tbody>
```

The resulting HTML output looks like this (notice the class attributes on the `tr` tags):

```
<tbody>
<tr class="row1"><th><a href="104/">This is a press release 51</a>
</th></tr>
<tr class="row2"><th><a href="103/">This is a press release 50</a>
</th></tr>
```

By overriding the styles for the `row1` and `row2` CSS selectors, we can use our own color scheme in the change list. We'll do that later in the chapter.

Inspecting the change_form.html template

We won't be working with this file. But if you want to add additional content above the form used to edit an object, this is the file you'd work with.

Customizing the admin header

To make our admin site feel less generic, we'll replace the default title and header at the top of the pages.

Create a new directory called admin under the directory `mycompany/templates`. Copy the `django/contrib/admin/templates/base_site.html` file to your `templates/admin` directory. This is the first file we'll be overriding.

Replacing the page title

In our admin pages, the page title is presented in this format:

```
<title>Site administration | Django site admin</title>
```

This can be changed by editing the `title` block in `base_site.html`. Open the `mycompany/templates/admin/site_base.html` file and edit the block that looks like this:

```
{% block title %}{{ title }} | {% trans 'Django site admin' %}{%
endblock %}
```

Replace the text in quotes after the pipe symbol with our site's title:

```
{% block title %}{{ title }} | {% trans 'MyCompany Administration'
%}{% endblock %}
```

 The `trans` tag is used by Django's internationalization (i18n) libraries to translate text into other languages. We're not going to translate our new text, but we'll leave the trans tags in the file in case you ever want to.

Point your browser to the URL `http://localhost:8000/admin/` and you will see that the title in the top of the browser window reflects our new change:

Changing the header text

The next thing we'll want to change is the text **Django administration**. We can do this by editing the contents of the `branding` block in the `base_site.html` file:

```
{% block branding %}
<h1 id="site-name">{% trans 'MyCompany administration' %}</h1>
{% endblock %}
```

Reload the page and you'll see that the header text has changed:

Adding a new link box to the admin

Let's add some links to the admin dashboard in a format that matches the way apps are listed. We'll add links to Google Analytics for our page traffic analysis and Google Webmaster tools to help get us indexed properly in Google. Having these links available in your admin page is handy when administering your site.

Overriding the admin index file

Copy the `django/contrib/admin/index.html` file to your `mycompany/templates/admin` directory. This page controls the appearance of the dashboard in the admin, so we'll be adding the links at its top.

When our apps are listed on this page, they appear automatically as part of the inner workings of the admin app. We don't want to alter this functionality as, when a new app is added in the future, we don't want to manually add it to the admin home page. By adding additional lines to the `index.html` file, we'll get our extra content added without changing the way the apps are loaded.

Look for the `content-main` div in the `templates/admin/index.html` file (around line 13):

```
{% block content %}
<div id="content-main">

{% if app_list %}
    {% for app in app_list %}
        <div class="module">
```

We're going to stick our additional content at the beginning of the `div` before the `{% if app_list %}` tag like this:

```
{% block content %}
<div id="content-main">

<p>This is where the extra content goes.</p>

{% if app_list %}
    {% for app in app_list %}
        <div class="module">
```

When we reload the page, you'll see the new text above the first app:

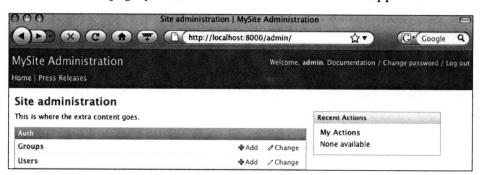

Rather than adding our new HTML code into the `index.html` file, let's use an include file instead to keep the code cleaner.

Edit `templates/admin/index.html` to use an include file:

```
{% block content %}
<div id="content-main">

{% include 'admin/index_links.html' %}

{% if app_list %}
    {% for app in app_list %}
```

Creating the include file

Create a new file at `templates/admin/index_links.html` and add this line:

```
<p>This is where the extra content goes.</p>
```

When you render the page, it should look exactly the way it did the last time. Now that we know it works, let's add some HTML markup so that the links are grouped in a look that matches the rest of the dashboard.

In `templates/admin/index_links.html`, replace the contents with this:

```
<style>
.module div {
  padding: 5px;
  font-weight: bold;
  border-bottom: 1px solid #eee;
  line-height: 13px;
}
.module div a {
  font-weight: bold;
}
</style>

<div class="module">
  <h2>Tool Links</h2>
  <div><a href="http://analytics.google.com">Google Analytics</a></
div>
  <div><a href="http://www.google.com/webmasters/tools/">Google
Webmaster Tools</a></div>
</div>
```

Let's break it down and explain a couple of pieces of markup:

- We apply the class `module` to the `div`. This gives the box the distinct look with the blue title bar.

- The `h2` tag becomes the text inside the box's blue title.

- We have a style block inside the include file, but you can put it anywhere you feel like.

When you reload the page, it should look like this:

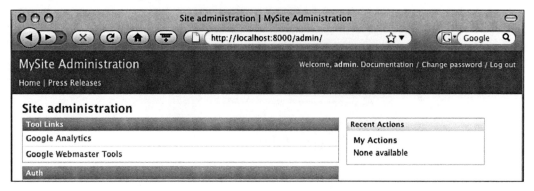

Customizing the admin color scheme

If you've ever looked at the admin page with CSS turned off, you'll know that it owes most of its beauty to the CSS stylesheets it ships with. Here's what it looks like without the styles applied:

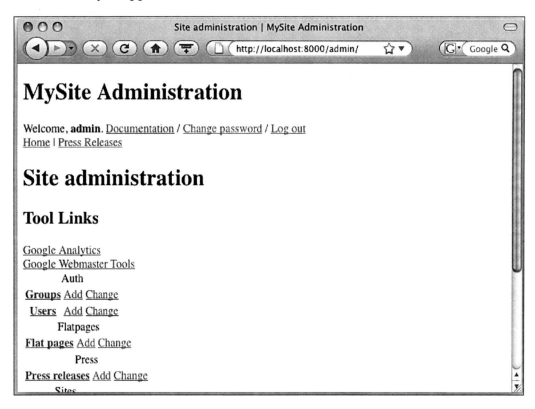

Rather than trying to edit the stylesheets directly, we'll just redefine the specific styles needed to apply our color scheme. We only need to override the specific properties we want to change, such as the font or the background color.

Identifying styles to change

The admin stylesheets are found in `django/contrib/admin/media/css`, but we don't need to copy them anywhere to make our changes. We just need to identify the selectors we'd like to override. We can do that by viewing the source on the rendered admin pages and seeing what the IDs and class attributes are applied to the content we want to change.

You can also use third-party tools to identify the CSS that is applied to elements on the page. Freely available tools such as Firebug and the Web Developer Toolbar for Firefox are very handy for this kind of work.

Firebug: `https://addons.mozilla.org/en-US/firefox/addon/1843`

Developer Toolbar: `https://addons.mozilla.org/en-US/firefox/addon/60`

For our customizations, we will change these admin page elements:

- Header background color (controlled by the `background-color` property of the `div` named `header`)
- Header title font color (controlled by the `color` property of the `h1` element in the `div` named `header`)
- Dashboard box header background color (controlled by the `background-color` and color selectors in the `module` class applied to `caption` and `h2` elements)
- Change list shaded row background color (controlled by the `background-color` property of the `row1` class)

Using the extrastyle block

Earlier in the chapter, we identified some special blocks the admin template authors put in the `base.html` template that allow us to add in extra functionality. The `extrastyle` block allows us to define CSS in our `base_site.html` template that we've already copied into our templates directory.

In `templates/admin/base_site.html`, add these lines:

```
{% block extrastyle %}
<style>
/* Header background color */
#header {
  background-color: #f57948;
}
/* Header title font color */
#branding h1 {
  color: #fff;
}
/* Link box title bar color */
.module caption, .module h2 {
  background-color: #f57948;
  background-image: None;
  color: #fff;
}
/* Change list shaded row color */
.row1 {
  background-color:#eee;
}
/* Change list non-shaded row color */
.row2 {
  background-color: #fff;
}
</style>
{% endblock %}
```

When the page is rendered, you can view the source and see that our `extrastyle` block has been injected into the top of the resulting HTML.

Since a picture is worth a thousand words, let's take a look at a labeled screenshot of what we just built. This printed page doesn't convey color well, but the labels should help us show what we just changed:

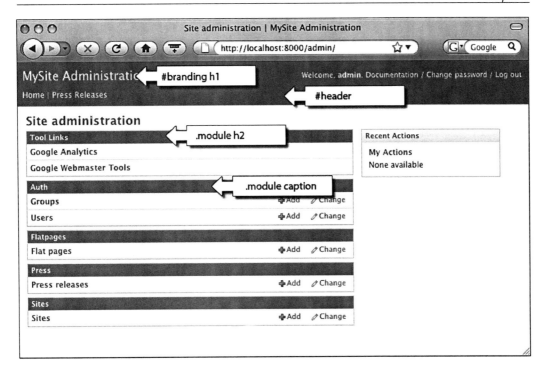

Here is what the admin change list page looks like with our CSS changes:

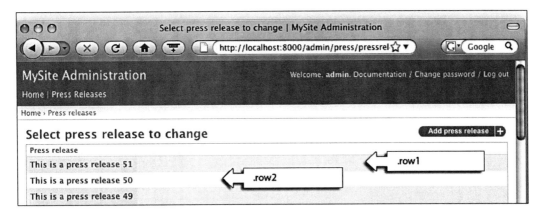

By adding some simple CSS to the extrastyle block, we were able to customize the admin stylesheets to fit the color scheme of our site.

Summary

In this chapter, we edited the templates of the Django admin application to add additional content and make the color scheme match our site.

We looked at the structure of the admin templates and how we can override them by creating an admin directory under our site's templates directory. We saw how the template filesystem loader will look for the files in this directory before looking at the template files under the admin application.

We explored how to change the admin header by editing the `base_site.html` file with our own information. We added our own links to the admin dashboard in a format that matches the other boxes on the page.

Finally, by using some special blocks in the admin base template, we added a set of global navigation links and the new CSS rules to override the default admin stylesheet.

In the next chapter, we'll look at how to improve performance using Django's caching libraries to cache our page content.

10
Caching Your Pages

The Django framework makes it easy to produce dynamic pages and generate content "on the fly" when a page is requested. Under certain circumstances, this can have a negative impact on your site's performance, such as when you start generating a large amount of traffic or if your pages use intensive database queries. In these situations, you can use the built-in caching mechanisms to reduce the amount of processing that goes into serving each request.

In this chapter, we will:

- Explore the basics of caching output
- Compare the different cache backends that Django offers
- Configure your site for caching
- Cache content on a per-view basis
- Cache content from within Django templates
- Use the low-level cache API to cache specific pieces of data
- Cache your entire site automatically
- Explore strategies for using different cache mechanisms together
- Configure Django to work with caches other than your own

An overview

Generating web pages for every request can be difficult for the server. But if we can hold on to data between requests and serve it again for the next request, we can reduce the overhead of serving each page.

We use a cache to store the result of a query so that future requests won't have to look it up again. Deciding how long to hold onto the data before looking it up again depends on your situation; but the longer you can go without having to look it up, the more performance you should be able to squeeze out of your server.

Do you need caching?

How do you know if you need to implement caching on your site? Usually, there are a few warning signs that indicate the time one should think about using caching such as:

- Processor or memory usage has climbed to a level that you are not comfortable with.
- Your web or database server cannot keep up with the incoming requests.
- It takes too long for the server to render a page request (the underlying page, not including images or external references).
- You anticipate your site traffic increasing to a point where one of the previous items will come into play.
- You want to be one of the cool kids who use caching on their site.

How caching works

Whether it's a complex database query, an intensive algorithm, or just the sheer number of incoming requests that are causing problems, caching can help your pages render more quickly. The concept is simple: Do the work once, and then save the results for the next time they are needed.

Holding on to the results can save time, but how long do you go without looking them up again? It depends on how often the underlying data changes. For example, if you're serving an hourly weather forecast, you may only need to look up the data once per hour. If you're serving current weather conditions, you'll probably have to look it up every 5 or 10 minutes.

What if you're serving the weather conditions for more than one city? You don't want to look up Atlanta's weather and serve it to someone looking for conditions in Dallas, and so you'll have to use a label to identify the piece of data. This label is what we'll call the **cache key**, and the conditions are the **cached data**. The amount of time spent before looking up the conditions again is the **cache expiration** or **cache timeout**. When the timeout is reached, the data is considered **stale** and won't be used anymore.

Exploring the available cache systems

The Django cache framework offers a variety of cache backends with a consistent interface. This gives you the flexibility to store your cached data as you see fit and change it later without having to change any of your code. For example, you can use the filesystem as the cache backend while your site is small, and upgrade to the Memcached backend later without having to change the code in your views.

Let's briefly look at the different cache backend options.

Filesystem caching

This backend saves the cached data to a file on the local filesystem. This is a great starter option for caching as it is easy to set up, works well on shared hosting environments, and doesn't rely on the database, thus reducing the number of reads and writes. You are limited, however, by the speed of reading and writing to the server's hard drive (also known as disk I/O).

Database caching

This backend uses a special database table to store its cached data. Like the filesystem backend, it works well in shared hosting environments and is easy to set up. But it is not good for environments where you are trying to keep down the number of database reads/writes, as it stores the data in a special database table.

Memcached

Memcached is a daemon that runs on the server and uses TCP/IP sockets for communication. It is considered to be the fastest, most efficient cache backend for Django (and many other frameworks as well). Memcached is an in-memory cache. It stores the cached data in RAM, avoiding the I/O overhead of the filesystem and database caches.

Memcached takes up the server RAM, so it usually isn't available in shared hosting situations. If you have a dedicated server and can spare the RAM, this is the best cache backend option. It has the added benefit that multiple servers can access the same cache, since it uses TCP/IP, and you can pool together separate Memcached servers to act as a single cache.

Another consideration when using this backend is that Python client libraries are required to use Memcached. They're freely available and easy to install.

 Memcached stores its data in RAM and all data is lost when the machine or the daemon restarts. This isn't a problem as you shouldn't store anything in cache that can't be regenerated.

Local memory caching

This backend (also known as locmem) is an alternative to Memcached, but at the time of this writing is not considered to be suitable for production sites. There are debates on the Django bug list about whether more than one web server process can access the same local memory space. Perhaps by the time you read this, the links will have been worked out. But for now, consider it as a development-only cache. (If you have the RAM available, just go with Memcached anyway!)

Dummy caching

This backend is designed for development work when you want to see fresh data on every request. It doesn't actually cache any data, but allows you to put your caching calls into place without getting errors saying you don't have a cache backend installed. Alternatively, you could set up one of the other cache backends and change the expiration time to zero seconds, ensuring that you always see new content; but this way is much cleaner.

Setting up your cache system

Now that you've seen the various cache backends that Django offers, we can now start implementing the code to work with them. Regardless of the backend you chose, the code will be identical.

Configuring the cache backend

To tell Django which backend we intend to use, we will set a variable called CACHE_BACKEND in our `mycompany/settings.py` file. Each backend uses a slightly different value, so we'll run through each separately.

Database caching

In order to use the database caching backend, you also have to run the `createcachetable` command from the `manage.py` file. This example uses `my_cache_table` as the name of the table, but you're free to use whatever you like:

```
$ python manage.py createcachetable my_cache_table
```

Once you have your cache table set up, add the backend to your `mycompany/settings.py` file:

```
CACHE_BACKEND = 'db://my_cache_table'
```

Filesystem caching

Filesystem caching requires very little setup, and the backend points to an absolute directory path on your filesystem. Make sure the web server process has permission to write and delete in that directory (the directory must exist).

There are three slashes at the beginning of the setting, and a trailing slash is not required:

```
CACHE_BACKEND = 'filesystem:///projects/mycompany/cache/'
```

Local memory caching

Local memory (locmem) caching requires no setup. You just provide this backend setting:

```
CACHE_BACKEND = 'locmem:///'
```

Dummy caching

Like locmem, dummy caching also uses a very simple setting:

```
CACHE_BACKEND = 'dummy:///'
```

Memcached

Memcached is the most complex backend setup, but it's not very difficult to set up. Make sure you install the Python library cmemcache (preferred) or python-memcached.

Once you have the Python libraries installed, the backend setting uses the server IP address and the port number. In this example, it's on the local machine (127.0.0.1) on port 11211, the standard port for Memcached:

```
CACHE_BACKEND = 'memcached://127.0.0.1:11211/'
```

Adding additional backend arguments

Once you have your backend configured, you can add some additional arguments to tailor the way it works:

- **timeout**: This is the amount of time that an item can be in cache before it's considered stale. The default value is 300 seconds.
- **max_entries**: This is the maximum number of entries that can build up in the cache before the cache is cleaned. The default value is 300 entries.
- **cull_percentage**: When the cache is cleaned, the cull percentage is the percentage of the entries that are removed when the maximum number of entries is reached.

The formats of the arguments are similar to URL querystring parameters:

```
CACHE_BACKEND = 'locmem:///?timeout=60&max_entries=300'
```

Setting up for the examples

You can use any of the cache backends for the examples that follow (except dummy, since it won't do anything). The easiest one to set up is probably the local memory cache, as it doesn't require you do to anything except add the backend configuration to your settings file.

Caching individual views

Now that you've configured caching, let's implement it in one of our views.
Our press release detail view is a great candidate for caching. The content of the individual releases rarely changes and, therefore, doesn't need to be queried from the database for every request.

We'll use the same view at the `mycompany/press/views.py` file that we've been using throughout our chapters. In Chapter 6, we added functionality to the view to work with multiple templates by adding the highlighted lines:

```
def detail(request, pid):
    '''
    Accepts a press release ID and returns the detail page
    '''
    p = get_object_or_404(PressRelease, id=pid)

    if request.GET.has_key('printable'):
        template_file = 'press/detail_printable.html'
    else:
        template_file = 'press/detail.html'

    t = loader.get_template(template_file)
    c = Context({'press': p})
    return HttpResponse(t.render(c))
```

Let's simplify the view so that we can just focus on learning how to work with caching. Strip out the extra lines and your view should look like this:

```
def detail(request, pid):
    '''
    Accepts a press release ID and returns the detail page
    '''
    p = get_object_or_404(PressRelease, id=pid)
    t = loader.get_template('press/cache_detail.html')
    c = Context({'press': p})
    return HttpResponse(t.render(c))
```

Notice that we have changed the name of the template that is loaded by the template loader to a new file called `cache_detail.html`. Create a new file called `cache_detail.html` in the `mycompany/templates/press` directory and add these lines:

```
<html>
<head>
<title>{{ press.title }}</title>
</head>
<body>
<h1>{{ press.title }}</h1>
<p>
<hr>Current Datetime: {% now "H:m:s" %}<hr>
Author: {{ press.author }}<br/>
Date: {{ press.pub_date }}<br/>
</p>
<p>
{{ press.body }}
</p>
</body>
</html>
```

Once you have these items in place, run your development server and test your setup. Your output should look similar to the screenshot, depending on the content of your press release.

Browse to `http://localhost:8000/press/detail/1/` and you should see something similar to this:

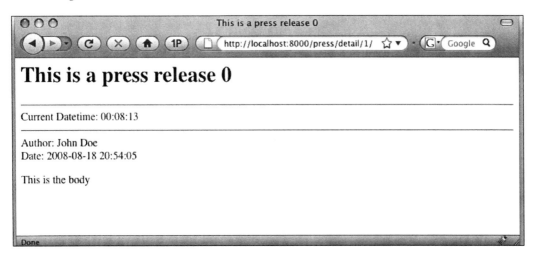

Reload the URL a couple of times, and make sure the current time changes for each reload.

Adding caching

Let's "freeze time" by adding caching to our view. Once in place, the result of the view will be saved in cache and the code inside the view won't be evaluated again until the cache expires. We can see that this behavior is working when we reload our view and the date and time do not change.

Add the highlighted lines to the `mycompany/press/views.py` file:

```
from django.views.decorators.cache import cache_page
def detail(request, pid):
    '''
    Accepts a press release ID and returns the detail page
    '''
    p = get_object_or_404(PressRelease, id=pid)
    t = loader.get_template('press/cache_detail.html')
    c = Context({'press': p})
    return HttpResponse(t.render(c))
detail = cache_page(detail, 10)
```

Alternatively, you can use Python's decorator syntax for caching if you're using Python version 2.4 or greater:

```
from django.views.decorators.cache import cache_page
@cache_page(10)
def detail(request, pid):
    '''
    ...
```

Load the page, view the results, and refresh the page. You'll see that the page content does not change when you refresh. Once the ten seconds have passed, the cache expires and the view runs again.

 It's usually a good idea to set the value of your cache timeout as a variable in your site's `settings.py` file and use it in your views. This will make it easier to change the cache timeout values in multiple views at once.

Caching pieces of templates

Django also gives us the ability to cache fragments of templates using a special template tag. We can use it to cache the part of the template that evaluates the current time.

Remove the line of code that caches the detail view and reload the page a few times to make sure the time is refreshing each time. Your `detail` view should look like this again:

```
def detail(request, pid):
    '''
    Accepts a press release ID and returns the detail page
    '''
    p = get_object_or_404(PressRelease, id=pid)
    t = loader.get_template('press/cache_detail.html')
    c = Context({'press': p})
    return HttpResponse(t.render(c))
```

Once you've reverted the view to it's pre-caching state, add the highlighted lines to `mycompany/templates/press/detail.html`:

```
<html>
<head>
<title>{{ press.title }}</title>
</head>
<body>
<h1>{{ press.title }}</h1>
<p>
{% load cache %}
{% cache 10 curtime %}
<hr>Current Datetime: {% now "H:m:s" %}<hr>
{% endcache %}
Author: {{ press.author }}<br/>
Date: {{ press.pub_date }}<br/>
</p>
<p>
{{ press.body }}
</p>
</body>
</html>
```

This new block loads a library called `cache` and uses the `cache` template tag. The tag takes two arguments: the length of time to cache the fragment, and a unique name for the fragment. In this example, it will be cached for 10 seconds and called `curtime`.

Test out the page and see if it works in the same way as it did when we used the per-view cache. Template fragment caching is great for pieces of content that get brought into your templates (such as with an include) or when you want very fine control over what content gets cached.

Low-level caching

If per-view and template caching don't solve your needs, Django offers you a way to choose exactly the pieces that get cached. The low-level cache API lets you read and write to and from the cache and explicitly decide how you want the data to be cached.

Say, for example, you wanted the press release to show the current date and time each refresh, but you don't want the database to get queried for the content of the release? You can use low-level caching to save the result of the database lookup.

Before we begin, remove the template fragment caching from the previous example by editing the highlighted line in `mycompany/templates/press/cache_detail.html`:

```
<html>
<head>
<title>{{ press.title }}</title>
</head>
<body>
<h1>{{ press.title }}</h1>
<p>
<hr>Current Datetime: {% now "H:m:s" %}<hr>
Author: {{ press.author }}<br/>
Date: {{ press.pub_date }}<br/>
</p>
<p>
{{ press.body }}
</p>
</body>
</html>
```

Verify that each refresh updates the time displayed on the page each time you hit refresh.

In the `mycompany/press/views.py` file, add the highlighted lines:

```python
from django.core.cache import cache

def detail(request, pid):
    '''
    Accepts a press release ID and returns the detail page
    '''
    cache_key= "press_release_%s" % pid
    p = cache.get(cache_key)

    if not p:
        p = get_object_or_404(PressRelease, id=pid)
```

```
        cache.set(cache_key, p, 60)

    t = loader.get_template('press/cache_detail.html')
    c = Context({'press': p})
    return HttpResponse(t.render(c))
```

Once you have the code in place, load the URL in the browser and verify the time increments each time you refresh. Go into the admin and change some of the values of your press release and reload it in the browser. You should see the time increment, but the data should remain unchanged. (The example above gives you 60 seconds to update the press release.)

What happened in this example to make it work? First, we created a cache key to act as a label for our data. It's important that we make sure the key is unique so we add the ID of the object as part of the key.

```
    cache_key= "press_release_%d" % pid
```

Next, we try to retrieve the object from the cache using the key. If it doesn't exist, the `cache.get()` method returns `None`.

```
    p = cache.get(cache_key)

    if not p:
        p = get_object_or_404(PressRelease, id=pid)
        cache.set(cache_key, p, 60)
```

If the `cache.get()` method returns `None`, we know that we have to look up the object. While we're looking it up, we set the value in the cache so the next request won't have to do this step.

 If the object does exist in cache but is expired, it's treated as if it didn't exist and the method returns `None`. We don't have to worry about checking if it exists and it's not stale—that's taken care of for us.

Caching your whole site

If you want to cache your entire site without having to configure the cache for each individual view, Django provides middleware that can do this for you.

Edit the MIDDLEWARE_CLASSES tuple in your `mycompany/settings.py` file to look like this: (add the highlighted lines)

```
MIDDLEWARE_CLASSES = (
    'django.middleware.common.CommonMiddleware',
    'django.middleware.cache.UpdateCacheMiddleware',
```

```
    'django.contrib.sessions.middleware.SessionMiddleware',
    'django.middleware.common.CommonMiddleware',
    'django.contrib.auth.middleware.AuthenticationMiddleware',
    'django.middleware.cache.FetchFromCacheMiddleware',
)
```

The order of the classes in the tuple is important, so make sure you add them exactly as listed. If you're not using all of these pieces of middleware and your tuple looks different, just make sure you put the highlighted lines around the CommonMiddleware element.

Add the following lines to your mycompany/settings.py file:

```
CACHE_MIDDLEWARE_SECONDS = 300
CACHE_MIDDLEWARE_KEY_PREFIX = 'mycompany_'
CACHE_MIDDLEWARE_ANONYMOUS_ONLY = True
```

You can probably figure out that CACHE_MIDDLEWARE_SECONDS is a global setting for the cache expiration time of all views. (Note that you cannot individually set different cache times for different views.) What do the other settings do?

The value of CACHE_MIDDLEWARE_KEY_PREFIX is prepended to the cache key that is automatically generated for a view. This ensures that if you have multiple sites running from the same code base (as we had in the chapter where we served our mobile and desktop sites from the same code) you won't have a key collision. When a key collision occurs, the output of one site's view overwrites another site's, resulting in erroneous output.

Finally, CACHE_MIDDLEWARE_ANONYMOUS_ONLY ensures that requests made by logged-in users don't get cached. This prevents user-specific data from getting written into the cache.

Consider the following snippet of template code:

```
Hello, {{ user.username }}!
```

If user "A" requests the page and it gets cached, user "B" will see the wrong username on the page.

> **Caution:** Even if you aren't serving user-specific data in your templates, Django's automatic admin interface requires the anonymous-only setting to work properly. If you forget to put it in, you'll update records and won't see the changes reflected in the admin until you clear the cache.

If you're testing the per-site cache and don't seem to get the pages to cache, make sure you're not logged in to the admin site!

Preventing data from being cached

If you're using the per-site cache and have some specific views that you want to exclude from cache, you can use the `never_cache` decorator:

```
from django.views.decorators.cache import never_cache

@never_cache
def detail(request, pid):
    ...
```

Using the `never_cache` decorator ensures that the view will not be cached by the per-site caching mechanism.

General caching strategies

With different caching mechanism options such as per-site, per-view, low-level, and so on, it may be difficult to determine which one fits your site best. There is no single "right" answer, but let's look at a general strategy for implementing caching on your site.

The per-site cache is fast and easy to implement. You don't have to remember to implement caching in your views, and you can configure the caching to prevent authenticated requests from getting cached.

What if you have views that require authentication? With the per-site cache enabled, these views won't get the benefit of the cache. In this case, you may want to implement low-level caching to store the bits of data that aren't user-specific. But sometimes, this isn't possible, for example when you present data specific to the logged-in user.

If you are presenting a lot of user-specific data, look for places in your templates where you can add caching, such as a dynamically generated menu or navigation system.

Keep in mind that not everything on your site will benefit from being cached. There is an overhead to implement the cache, and if it's greater than the overhead of executing the code in question, you probably won't experience any benefit.

Working with outside caches

Not every cache you'll deal with is stored locally on your server. For example, many web browsers have built-in functionality to cache content and some networks are behind proxies and web accelerators.

We can provide some additional information via HTTP headers to these caches that make sure our content is stored properly. Specifically, the `Vary` HTTP header allows us to tell a cache how to differentiate content that it might otherwise think is the same.

As a simple example, we can tell a cache to cache content that is based on the user agent that a visitor is using. This lets us cache a request for a mobile device, such as an iPhone, differently than we would for a generic mobile device.

```
from django.views.decorators.vary import vary_on_headers

@vary_on_headers('User-Agent')
def detail(request, pid):
    ...
```

If you'd like to try it out, you can do so if you have two web different web browsers. Point your first browser at the page and it will cache the content. Point your second browser at the page, and you will not see the cached results because the browser's user agent string will be different.

You can tell the cache to vary on a variety of criteria: user agents, visitor language preferences, cookies, and so on. The `vary_on_headers` decorator allows you to pass multiple values to it.

If varying your content for upstream caches is important to the proper operation of your site, check the online documentation for a full discussion and more examples.

 Make sure you remove the middleware caching libraries or set the cache expiration time to zero seconds if you're going on to the next chapter or you will be working with cached pages!

Summary

In this chapter, we explored how to improve the performance of our site by implementing caching. We saw the different backends that Django offers and learned how to configure our site to use each of them. We also learned how to cache pieces of data using the low-level API, the output of views with per-view caching, and even our whole site with per-site caching.

We looked at when certain cache mechanisms work better than others and also the general caching strategies. Finally, we wrapped up by looking at how our data might be cached by outside servers and how to make sure our data is served properly in those situations.

In the next chapter, we will look at serving your site in multiple languages with Django's internationalization (i18n) libraries.

11
Internationalization

Internationalization, also known as **i18n** (the word "internationalization" consists of the letters "i" and "n" with 18 letters in between), provides a way to present your site in multiple languages from the same template files. Instead of creating a separate site in a different language, you identify strings of text in your templates that are substituted with a string in the appropriate language for the visitor.

In this chapter, we will:

- Learn how i18n works
- Build a sample application
- Configure the project for i18n
- Install the appropriate libraries to create language files
- Mark strings in our template for translation
- Create English and German translations for our project
- Learn how to manually and automatically configure language preference

Exploring i18n

Internationalization can be used to offer your site in multiple languages from a single project. Instead of creating multiple domains, projects, or templates, you can provide translation strings in your templates that allow for the appropriate language file to be chosen.

 One important thing to keep in mind is that the database content is not stored in multiple versions. It is presented to the user in the same way regardless of language. Saving multiple translations of content can be done, but it isn't something than can easily be done inside templates and so it's beyond the scope of this book.

When a user first views the site, an HTTP header called `Accept-Language` will identify his or her language preference. If it's not specified, Django will look at your project's settings file and see what the default language to serve is. You can also provide links to set cookies that Django will look for to determine the language preference.

In order to use i18n, we will have to tell Django that we are planning to use it, create a sample project with marked translation strings, create the translation files, and then view our templates. We'll configure Django to use the `Accept-Language` header later in the chapter. For now, we'll manually configure the language preference.

Creating an example application

To explore the concepts in this chapter, we'll need to create a sample application. We'll make a simple contact list application that displays a user's first name, last name, birthday, and salutation based on gender. This simple example will give us the ability to change the labels for the fields as well as the date format used to show the birthday and the language used to display the salutation.

For this example project, we'll assume you are following along with the book and working in the Django project called `mycompany`. If you are not, make the appropriate changes in the code for your project name. (You won't need any of the other apps we've built to follow along with this chapter.)

Start by adding a new application to your project. In the `/projects/mycompany` directory, run the following command:

```
$ python manage.py startapp contactlist
```

Once the app has been created, edit `mycompany/contactlist/models.py` to look like this:

```python
from django.db import models

GENDER = (
    (1, 'Male'),
    (2, 'Female'),
)


class Entry(models.Model):
    first_name = models.CharField(max_length=100)
    last_name = models.CharField(max_length=100)
    birthday = models.DateTimeField()
    gender = models.SmallIntegerField(choices=GENDER)

    def get_absolute_url(self):
```

```
        return "/contactlist/detail/%d/" % self.id

    class Meta:
        verbose_name_plural = 'entries'

    def __unicode__(self):
        return "%s, %s" % (self.last_name, self.first_name)
```

Once the model has been created, add the new app to the INSTALLED_APPS tuple in mycompany/settings.py. Add the highlighted line:

```
INSTALLED_APPS = (
    'django.contrib.auth',
    'django.contrib.admin',
    'django.contrib.contenttypes',
    'django.contrib.sessions',
    'django.contrib.sites',
    'mycompany.contactlist',
)
```

 You may have more applications installed if you've been keeping up with the book, which is OK — just add the highlighted entry to the tuple.

While in the mycompany/settings.py file, find the LANGUAGE_CODE setting and set it to en:

```
LANGUAGE_CODE = 'en'
```

Run the syncdb command in the root directory of the project to create the new model's database table:

```
$ python manage.py syncdb
```

Let's use the Django shell to quickly add a few entries to the application:

```
$ python manage.py shell
>>> from contactlist.models import Entry
>>>
>>> e = Entry.objects.create(first_name='John', last_name='Doe',
gender=1, birthday='1985-01-01')
>>>
>>> e = Entry.objects.create(first_name='Jane', last_name='Smith',
gender=2, birthday='1980-05-01')
```

With the model and data in place, add an entry to your `mycompany/urls.py` file to direct requests to our application. Add the following highlighted line:

```
urlpatterns = patterns('',
    (r'^admin/(.*)', admin.site.root),
    (r'^contact/', include('contactlist.urls')),
)
```

 Your root `urls.py` file may have more entries in it if you've been working with other chapters. That's not a problem; just add the highlighted entry to the list.

Create a new `urls.py` file in the `mycompany/contactlist/` directory and add the lines given in the code that follows. Notice that we are using generic views to display the list and detail for entry records in the highlighted lines:

```
from django.conf.urls.defaults import *
from contactlist.models import Entry

info_dict = {
    'queryset': Entry.objects.all(),
}

urlpatterns = patterns('django.views.generic.list_detail',
    (r'^(?P<object_id>[0-9]+)/$',
        'object_detail', info_dict),
    (r'^$', 'object_list', info_dict),
)
```

Finally, create template files for the list and detail views. We'll hard-code the English labels for now so that we can verify it's working.

Create a new directory called `contactlist` in the `mycompany/templates` directory. In `mycompany/templates/contactlist` add a new file called `entry_list.html` with the following lines:

```
<h1>Contact List</h1>
<ol>
{% for object in object_list %}
  <li><a href="/contact/{{ object.id }}">{{ object }}</a></li>
{% endfor %}
</ol>
```

Create a new file called `entry_detail.html` in the `mycompany/templates/contactlist/` directory and add the following lines:

```
<h1>Contact Information</h1>
<h2>
{% ifequal object.get_gender_display "Male" %}
```

```
  Mr.
{% else %}
  Mrs.
{% endifequal %}
{{ object.first_name }} {{ object.last_name }}
</h2>
<p>
First Name: {{ object.first_name }}<br/>
Last Name: {{ object.last_name }}<br/>
Birthday: {{ object.birthday|date:"m/d/Y" }}<br/>
</p>
```

Launch the development web server and verify that you see the correct the output for the two views. Browse to the URL `http://localhost:8000/contact/` and you should see this:

Browse to the URL `http://localhost:8000/contact/1/` and you should see this:

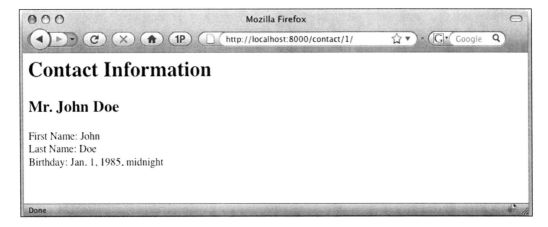

Congratulations! We now have a working project with which to test i18n.

Configuring your project for i18n

Now that our project is in place, let's tell Django that we are planning to use i18n in it. We'll start by adding some configuration settings.

In the `mycompany/settings.py` file, find the `LANGUAGE_CODE` setting and add an additional commented line for the German language setting `de`:

```
LANGUAGE_CODE = 'en'
#LANGUAGE_CODE = 'de'
```

These settings will tell Django that our project's default language is English, but the commented line will make it easy for us to switch the site to German for testing later.

While you're still in the file, make sure we're loading the internationalization machinery. (It's set to `True` by default, but make sure.)

```
USE_I18N = True
```

We'll need to create a directory where the i18n files are kept. Create a directory called `locale` in the `mycompany` folder at the root of your project:

```
$ mkdir /projects/mycompany/locale
```

Installing libraries for i18n translation

Before we can have the fun of creating different translations, we need to make sure our installation has the tools necessary to create the files needed for translation.

On Mac and Linux, Django uses the GNU *gettext* libraries. On Windows, you'll need to install *gettext for Windows*, available on Sourceforge at the URL `http://gnuwin32.sourceforge.net/packages/gettext.htm`.

Try the following command to see if you have the libraries installed properly. (The `cd` command is included to make sure you're running it from the root of your project, thus saving you from frustrating errors in case you forget.)

```
$ cd /projects/mycompany/
$ django-admin.py makemessages -l en
```

 `django-admin.py` is located in the `django/bin` directory. If it's not in your path, you will have to specify the full path to the file to run the command.

If you get no error, you are ready to continue. If you get an error saying that the libraries are not installed properly, do a web search for "gettext [*operating system*]" (inserting your operating system) and follow the instructions specific to your setup.

Marking strings as translatable

With all the prep work out of the way, let's modify the templates we created to be multilingual. Instead of the hardcoded English text that we put in our file earlier, let's start marking the field labels as translation strings. Basically, we're using a Django template tag to say "insert the translation here".

The list template is easy to work with as we only have to make two replacements. Replace the highlighted lines in `templates/contactlist/entry_list.html`:

```
{% load i18n %}
<h1>{% trans "Contact List" %}</h1>
<ol>
{% for object in object_list %}
  <li><a href="/contact/{{ object.id }}">{{ object }}</li>
{% endfor %}
</ol>
```

The first line loads the library file for internationalization, in the same way as loading any tag library. The second line is where we mark the text `Contact List` as a translation string.

Our changes haven't done much and if you view the URL in a browser, nothing will appear to have changed. Now that there is a translation string identified in a template, we can put the i18n mechanisms to work.

Creating message files

A message file is a plain-text file that contains all the named translation strings and how they should appear in a given language. Each language you choose to support will get its own message file.

To create a message file, we use the `django-admin.py` script. **Make sure you have created the locale directory in your project root** before doing this. (We covered this in an earlier step.) Navigate to your project root and use the script to make a message file:

```
$ cd /projects/mycompany/

$ django-admin.py makemessages -l en
```

We're telling the `makemessages` command to create a language file for `en` (English). Recall that in our `settings.py` file we defined this as the default language by setting it as the `LANGUAGE_CODE`.

Look in your `mycompany/locale` directory, and you will see a series of nested directories have been created. In the `mycompany/locale/en/LC_MESSAGES` directory, you'll find a file called `django.po`. This is the message file that was created.

Here's an excerpt from `mycompany/locale/en/LC_MESSAGES/django.po`:

```
#: templates/contactlist/entry_list.html:3
msgid "Contact List"
msgstr ""
```

Notice that the commented line tells you in what file and at what line number the translation string was found.

The `msgid` is the unique identifier for the translation string so don't change it. Also, make sure when you are adding more strings later that you don't create another one with the same name, as they must be unique.

The `msgstr` is blank. It's the translated text that will be displayed when the template is output. Since it's blank, Django will just use the value of `msgid`.

Let's put a value in `msgstr` so that we can see how it works. Open the file `mycompany/locale/en/LC_MESSAGES/django.po` and find the `entry_list.html` entry. Edit the highlighted line:

```
#: templates/contactlist/entry_list.html:3
msgid "Contact List"
msgstr "All Contacts"
```

Save the file, and use the `django-admin.py` script to run the `compilemessages` command from our project root directory:

```
$ cd /projects/mycompany/
$ django-admin.py compilemessages -l en
```

The script creates a `django.mo` file in the same folder as the message file — this is the compiled message file. (Don't try to view it; it's a binary file.)

 Important: Before you can see your changes reflected in a browser, you must restart your web server, **including the development server**.

Browse to the URL `http://localhost:8000/contact/` and you should see the new header:

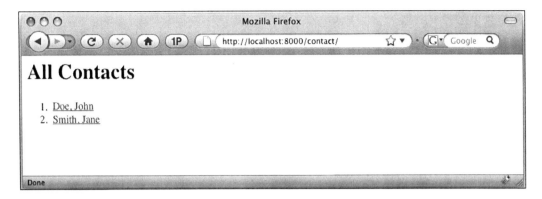

Notice the new translation "All Contacts" has replaced the "Contact List" text.

Let's create another message file for German translations. Using the `django-admin.py` script, run the `makemessages` command to create a German language file:

```
$ cd /projects/mycompany/
$ django-admin.py makemessages -l de
```

You'll see that a new directory has been created at `mycompany/locale/de`, almost identical to the `en` directory that was created earlier.

Find the `django.po` file in `mycompany/locale/de/LC_MESSAGES`, and make a German translation for the English text "Contact List" by adding the text in the highlighted line:

```
#: templates/contactlist/entry_list.html:3
msgid "Contact List"
msgstr "Alle Kontakts"
```

Save the file and use the `django-admin.py` script to run the `compilemessages` command:

```
$ cd /projects/mycompany/
$ django-admin.py compilemessages -l de
```

Alternatively, you can run the command with no argument to tell it to compile all message files:

```
$ django-admin.py compilemessages
```

In order to see our German translation, we need to go into our settings file and configure the default language for the site to German.

In the `mycompany/settings.py` file, edit the `LANGUAGE_CODE` lines to look like this:

```
#LANGUAGE_CODE = 'en'
LANGUAGE_CODE = 'de'
```

Restart your web server, and browse to the URL `http://localhost:8000/contact/` to see the German header:

Now that we've worked with the list template, let's mark translation strings in our detail template file. In the `mycompany/templates/contactlist/entry_detail.html` file, edit the content to look like this:

```
{% load i18n %}
<h1>{% trans 'Contact Information' %}</h1>
<h2>
{% ifequal object.get_gender_display "Male" %}
  {% trans "Mr." %}
{% else %}
  {% trans "Mrs." %}
{% endifequal %}
{{ object.first_name }} {{ object.last_name }}
</h2>
<p>
{% trans "First Name" %}: {{ object.first_name }}<br/>
{% trans "Last Name" %}: {{ object.last_name }}<br/>
{% trans "Birthday" %}:
{{ object.birthday|date:_("DATETIME_FORMAT") }}<br/>
</p>
```

There's nothing in here we haven't done yet, but the date formatting probably needs a little explanation. Because the European dates are formatted differently than they are in the United States, we need to mark the argument to the `date` filter as a translation string.

To do this, we use the `_()` function to tell Django that this is a translation string:

```
_("DATETIME_FORMAT")
```

It looks funny, but `_()` is a shortcut to the `django.utils.translation.gettext()` function that does i18n translation. Using this as an argument to the `date` filter allows us to translate the string before it is passed to the filter.

With these translation strings in place, run the `django-admin.py makemessages` command. Use the `-a` flag to tell it to remake all message files, looking for new translation strings in our templates:

```
$ cd /projects/mycompany/
$ django-admin.py makemessages -a
```

Look at the `django.po` files in the `en` and `de` directories. You'll find your new translation strings in the file, and notice that the translation we did for "Contact List" is still present—it was not overwritten by the `makemessages` command.

In the file `mycompany/locale/de/LC_MESSAGES/django.po`, add these translation strings to the highlighted lines:

```
#: templates/contactlist/entry_detail.html:3
msgid "Contact Information"
msgstr "Kontakt"
#: templates/contactlist/entry_detail.html:7
msgid "Mr."
msgstr "Herr"
#: templates/contactlist/entry_detail.html:9
msgid "Mrs."
msgstr "Frau"
#: templates/contactlist/entry_detail.html:16
msgid "First Name"
msgstr "Namen"
#: templates/contactlist/entry_detail.html:17
msgid "Last Name"
msgstr "Nachname"
#: templates/contactlist/entry_detail.html:18
msgid "Birthday"
msgstr "Geburtstag"
#: templates/contactlist/entry_detail.html:18
```

```
msgid "DATETIME_FORMAT"
msgstr "d/m/Y"
#: templates/contactlist/entry_list.html:3
msgid "Contact List"
msgstr "Alle Kontakts"
```

With the translations in place, run the compile messages command:

```
$ cd /projects/mycompany/
```

```
$ django-admin.py compilemessages
```

Restart your web server, and browse to `http://localhost:8000/contact/1/` to
see our changes:

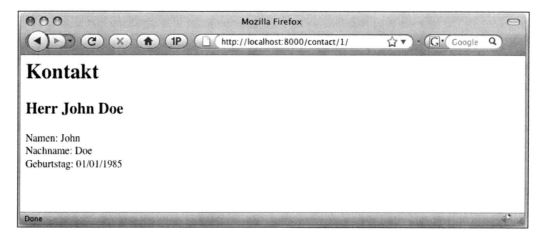

Notice that our new German translation messages are displayed in the template
output. If you switch the language back to `en` in your settings file, it will be displayed
in English. This works well when we want to decide the language to display, but
let's take it a step further and allow the user to tell us what language he or she wants
to see.

Enabling automatic language preference

In our examples we used the LANGUAGE_CODE setting to choose the default language
for our site. Let's configure our project to automatically determine the user's
language preference from their browser.

We can detect the user's language preference by inspecting the Accept-Language
HTTP header. Luckily, Django makes it very simple to inspect and take action based
on the header.

In your `mycompany/settings.py` file, add a special piece of middleware called `LocaleMiddleware` to your `MIDDLEWARE_CLASSES` tuple by adding the highlighted line:

```
MIDDLEWARE_CLASSES = (
    'django.contrib.sessions.middleware.SessionMiddleware',
    'django.middleware.locale.LocaleMiddleware',
    'django.middleware.common.CommonMiddleware',
    'django.contrib.auth.middleware.AuthenticationMiddleware',
)
```

If the classes listed in your project are slightly different, that's OK. Just make sure you add `LocaleMiddleware` after the `SessionMiddleware` entry. The order is important because Django stores the user's language preference as a part of its session, so the session middleware needs to come first.

 Important: If you are using cache middleware, make sure it comes before the locale middleware; otherwise, your users might get cached content in the wrong language!

While you are in the `settings.py` file, ensure the main language is set to English:

```
LANGUAGE_CODE = 'en'
```

In order to test the middleware, we need to configure our browser to send a different language header. Most browsers have a mechanism for setting the language preference. Here are a few examples:

- Firefox: **Preferences | Content | Languages**
- Internet Explorer: **Tools | Internet Options | General | Languages**
- Safari (on Mac): **System Preferences | International | Language**

With your main site language set to English (en), configure your browser's language preference to German (de). Browse to one of the pages, and you should see the German translations. Set it back to English, browse to the page, and you should see the English translations. With this working, the user's web browser can automatically tell Django in what language to present the content.

How Django determines language preference

When taking requests and returning content, Django goes through four steps to determine the visitor's language preference:

1. It looks in the user's session object for a key called `django_language`.

2. It looks for a cookie named `django_language` (or whatever you named it, if you changed the cookie name in your settings file).

3. It looks for the browser's `Accept-Language` HTTP header.

4. If none of those were found, it uses the `LANGUAGE_CODE` setting in your `settings.py` file.

Summary

If you need to offer your site in multiple languages, you can do so by using the internationalization (i18n) libraries built into the Django framework. Instead of creating another version of your site in a different language, you can translate strings in your templates depending on the user's language preferences or your site's configuration settings.

To enable i18n, you must configure your project by ensuring that `USE_I18N` is set to `True` and defining a `LANGUAGE_CODE` for your site. In your templates, load the `i18n` tag library and mark strings as translatable by putting them inside a `{% trans %}` tag. Run the `django-admin.py` script to make message files, then create your translations in those files, and run the script again to compile the message files.

To automatically choose the user's language preference based on his or her browser settings, load the `LocaleMiddleware` after any cache or session middleware in your site's settings file.

This chapter only scratches the surface of what Django is able to do with i18n. For more information, and for information on using i18n in your view code, consult the online documentation.

That concludes our book on Django templates and output. We've looked at a wide range of material, and hopefully you've learned a lot along the way. The best way to turn this new knowledge into a skill is through repetition. So review the material and practice, practice, practice!

Index

F

G

get_digit filter
  applying 81
  using 81

H

HTTP Response, view 37

I

i18n
  about 231
  exploring 231, 232
  libraries, installing for translation 236
  message files, creating 237-242
  project configuration 236
  sample application, creating 232-235
  strings, marking as translatable 237
ifchanged tag
  example 106
  using 105
ifequal tag
  example 107
  using 106
if tag
  using 104, 105
Ijust filter
  applying 85
  using 84
include tag
  example 107
  SSI, using 141
  using 107, 140
internationalization. *See* i18n
iriencode filter
  use 81

J

join filter
  applying 82
  using 81

L

last filter
  applying 82
  using 82

length_is filter
  applying 83
  using 83
length filter
  applying 82
  using 82
linebreaksbr filter
  applying 84
linebreaks filter
  applying 83
  using 83
linenumbers filter
  applying 84
  using 84
load tag
  example 108
  using 108
lower filter
  applying 85
  using 85

M

make_list filter
  applying 86
  using 86
Memcached, cache systems
  about 219
  features 219
message files
  creating 237-242
  creating, django-admin.pyscript used 237
mobile sites
  middleware file, installing 159, 160
  middleware file, settings used 160
  middleware file, writing 156, 157
  mobile devices, detecting 155, 156
  potential downsides 158
  redirecting to 155
  session variable, using 158
multiple child templates
  inheriting from 134
  three-level setup, adding 134-136
my company press release example
  setting up 145-147

**Thank you for buying
Django 1.0 Template
Development**

Packt Open Source Project Royalties

When we sell a book written on an Open Source project, we pay a royalty directly to that project. Therefore by purchasing Django 1.0 Template Development, Packt will have given some of the money received to the Django Project.

In the long term, we see ourselves and you—customers and readers of our books—as part of the Open Source ecosystem, providing sustainable revenue for the projects we publish on. Our aim at Packt is to establish publishing royalties as an essential part of the service and support a business model that sustains Open Source.

If you're working with an Open Source project that you would like us to publish on, and subsequently pay royalties to, please get in touch with us.

Writing for Packt

We welcome all inquiries from people who are interested in authoring. Book proposals should be sent to author@packtpub.com. If your book idea is still at an early stage and you would like to discuss it first before writing a formal book proposal, contact us; one of our commissioning editors will get in touch with you.

We're not just looking for published authors; if you have strong technical skills but no writing experience, our experienced editors can help you develop a writing career, or simply get some additional reward for your expertise.

About Packt Publishing

Packt, pronounced 'packed', published its first book "Mastering phpMyAdmin for Effective MySQL Management" in April 2004 and subsequently continued to specialize in publishing highly focused books on specific technologies and solutions.

Our books and publications share the experiences of your fellow IT professionals in adapting and customizing today's systems, applications, and frameworks. Our solution-based books give you the knowledge and power to customize the software and technologies you're using to get the job done. Packt books are more specific and less general than the IT books you have seen in the past. Our unique business model allows us to bring you more focused information, giving you more of what you need to know, and less of what you don't.

Packt is a modern, yet unique publishing company, which focuses on producing quality, cutting-edge books for communities of developers, administrators, and newbies alike. For more information, please visit our website: www.PacktPub.com.

Learning Website Development with Django

ISBN: 978-1-847193-35-3 Paperback: 264 pages

A beginner's tutorial to building web applications, quickly and cleanly, with the Django application framework

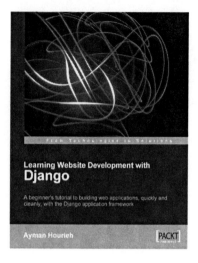

1. Create a complete Web 2.0-style web application with Django

2. Learn rapid development and clean, pragmatic design

3. Build a social bookmarking application

4. No knowledge of Django required

Expert Python Programming

ISBN: 978-1-847194-94-7 Paperback: 350 pages

Best practices for designing, coding, and distributing your Python software

1. Learn Python development best practices from an expert, with detailed coverage of naming and coding conventions

2. Apply object-oriented principles, design patterns, and advanced syntax tricks

3. Manage your code with distributed version control

4. Profile and optimize your code

5. Proactive test-driven development and continuous integration

Please check **www.PacktPub.com** for information on our titles

Practical Plone 3

ISBN: 978-1-847191-78-6   Paperback: 350 pages

A Beginner's Guide to Building Powerful Websites

1. Get a Plone-based website up and running quickly without dealing with code

2. Beginner's guide with easy-to-follow instructions and screenshots

3. Learn how to make the best use of Plone's out-of-the-box features

4. Customize security, look-and-feel, and many other aspects of Plone

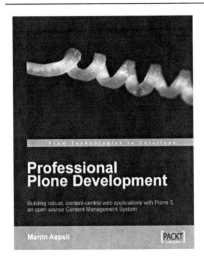

Professional Plone Development

ISBN: 978-1-847191-98-4   Paperback: 398 pages

Building robust, content-centric web applications with Plone 3, an open source Content Management System

1. Plone development fundamentals

2. Customizing Plone

3. Developing new functionality

4. Real-world deployments

Please check **www.PacktPub.com** for information on our titles

Printed in the United Kingdom by
Lightning Source UK Ltd., Milton Keynes
137364UK00001B/81-84/P